**AMSCO PUBLICATIONS**
A PART OF THE MUSIC SALES GROUP

LONDON / NEW YORK / LOS ANGELES / NASHVILLE / PARIS / SYDNEY / COPENHAGEN / BERLIN / MADRID / TOKYO

Published by
**Amsco Publications**
257 Park Avenue South, New York, NY10010, United States Of America.

Exclusive Distributors:
**Music Sales Limited**
Distribution Centre, Newmarket Road, Bury St Edmunds,
Suffolk, IP33 3YB, UK.
**Music Sales Corporation**
257 Park Avenue South, New York, NY10010, United States Of America.
**Music Sales Pty Limited**
120 Rothschild Avenue, Rosebery, NSW 2018, AUSTRALIA.

Order No. AM986744
ISBN-10: 1-84609-703-7
ISBN-13: 978-1-84609-703-4



Music Processed by Camden Music
Compiled by Heather Slater
Printed in the United States of America.

# Contents

# Anvil Chorus
## (from 'Il trovatore')

Composed by Giuseppe Verdi

Arranged by Jeremy Birchall

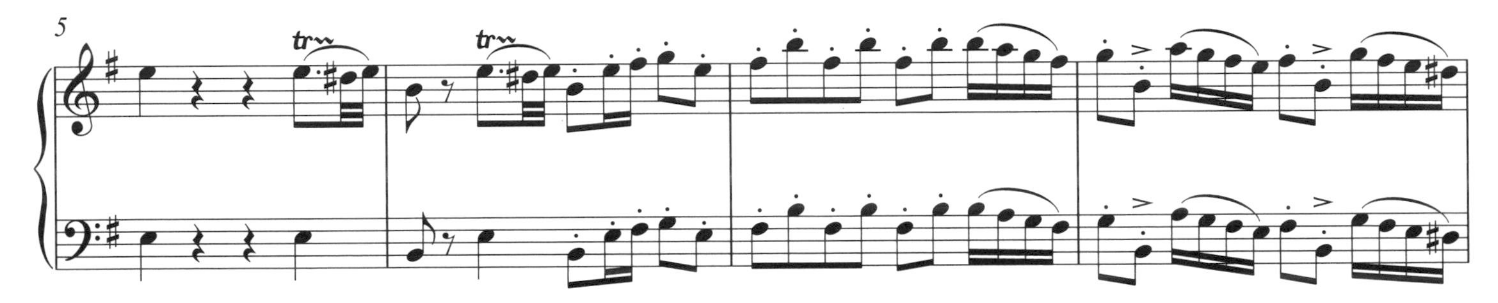

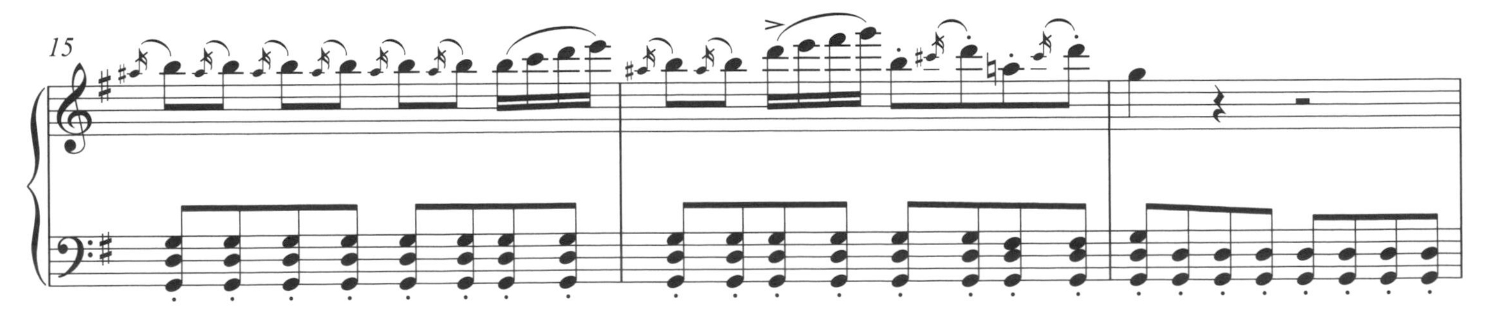

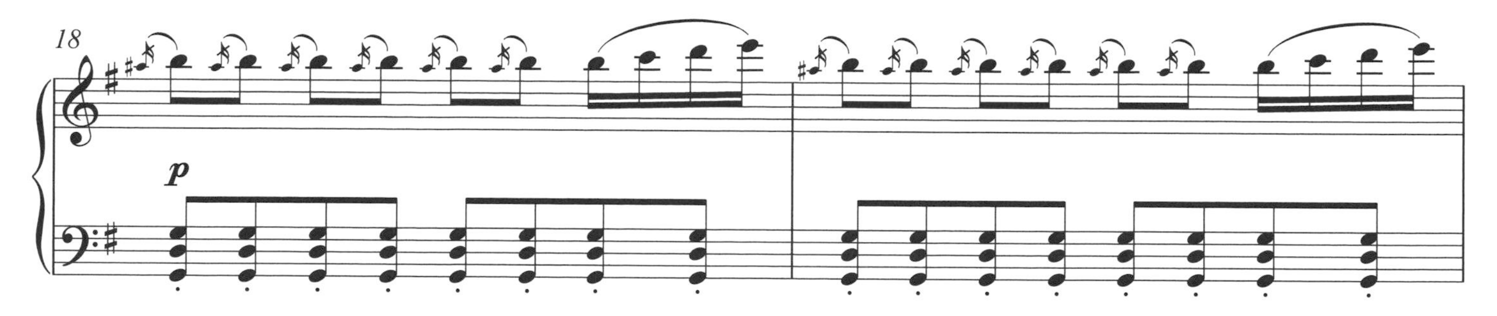
18
p

20
pp

24
tr
pp
tr

29

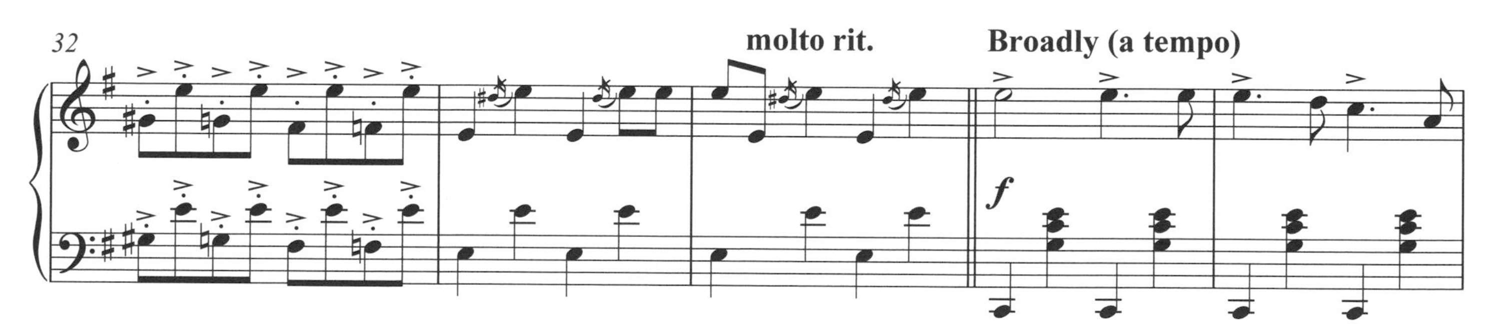
32
molto rit.
Broadly (a tempo)
f

37

43

48
tr
tr
ff
f

52
tr
tr

56
tr

59
tr
p
rit.

62
a tempo

64
pp

68
tr

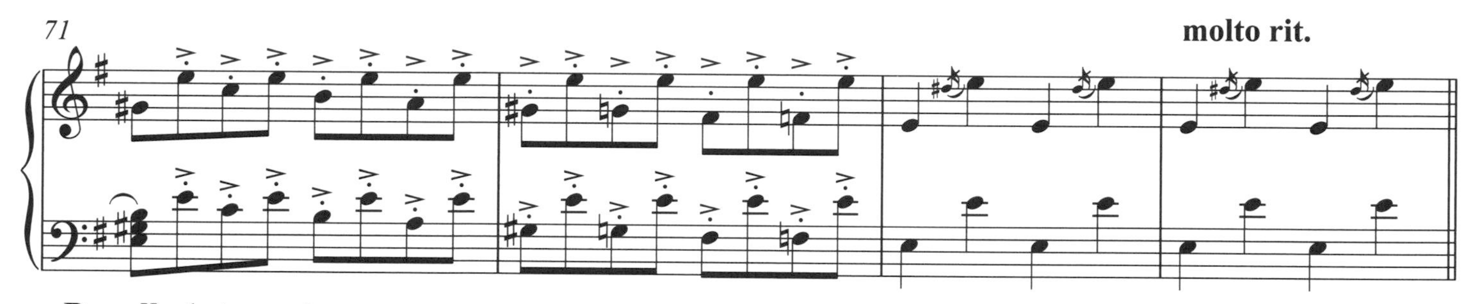
71
molto rit.

Broadly (a tempo)
75
ff

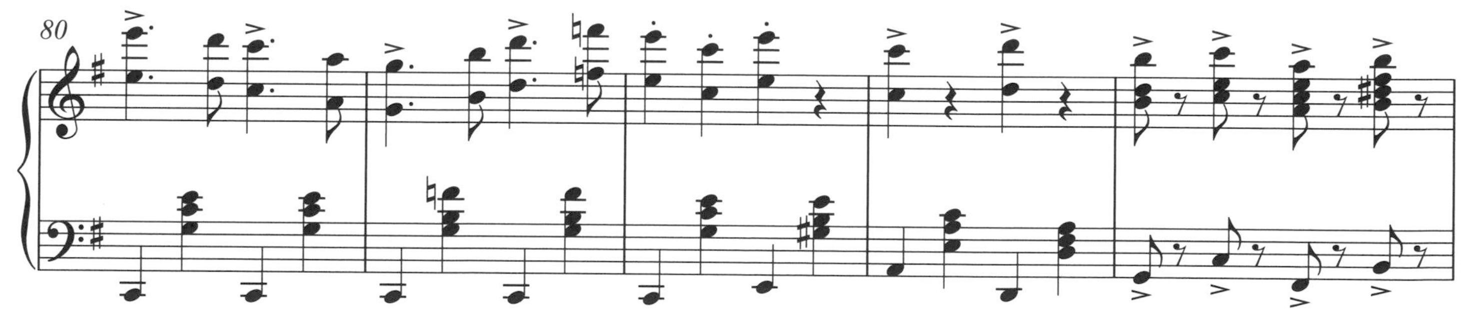
80

85
ff

# THE BARBER OF SEVILLE

## (OVERTURE)

Composed by Gioachino Rossini

Arranged by Quentin Thomas

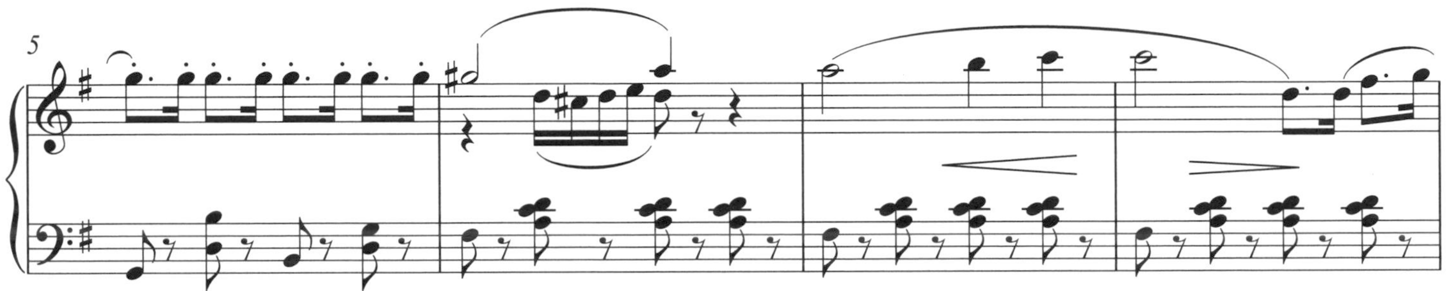

21
3
3

25
3
3
3
3

29
sim.

33
sub. mp

37
cresc.

41
f e cresc.

45
3
3
3

49
ff
sub. p
mp
pp
mp

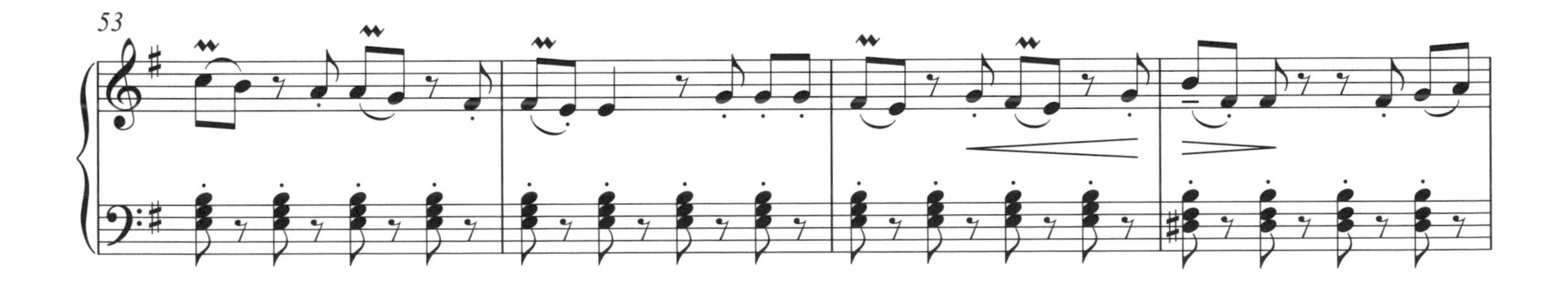
53

57
f
p

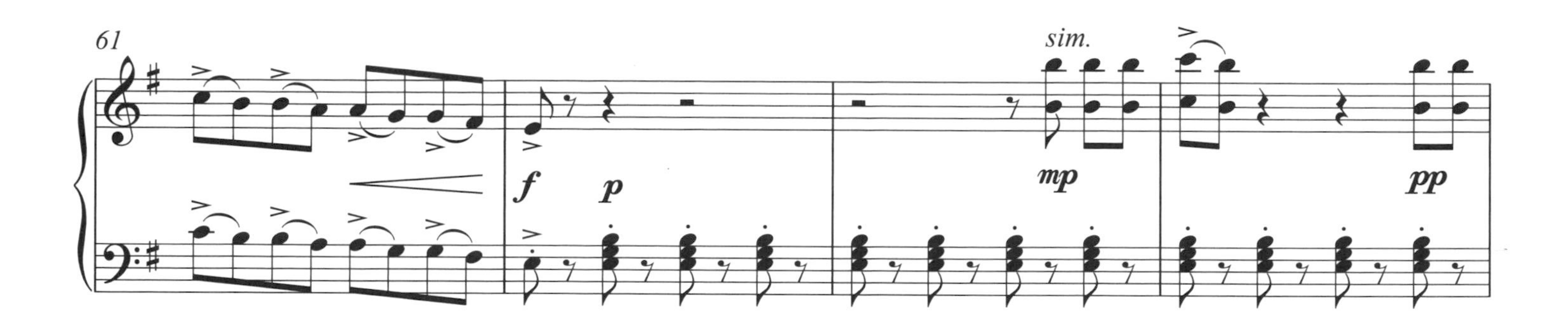
61
sim.
f
p
mp
pp

65
mp

69
molto cresc.

72
f

75
ff

# Bridal Chorus
## (from 'Lohengrin')

Composed by Richard Wagner

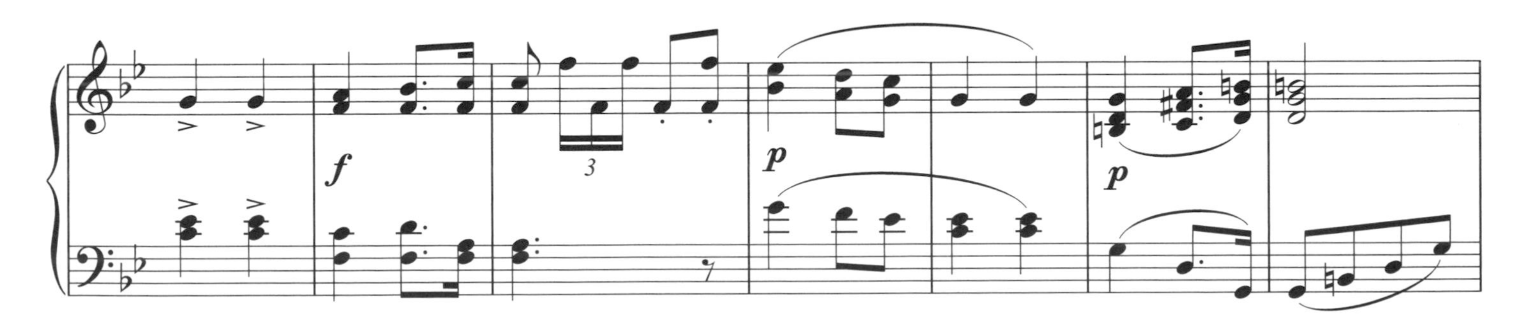

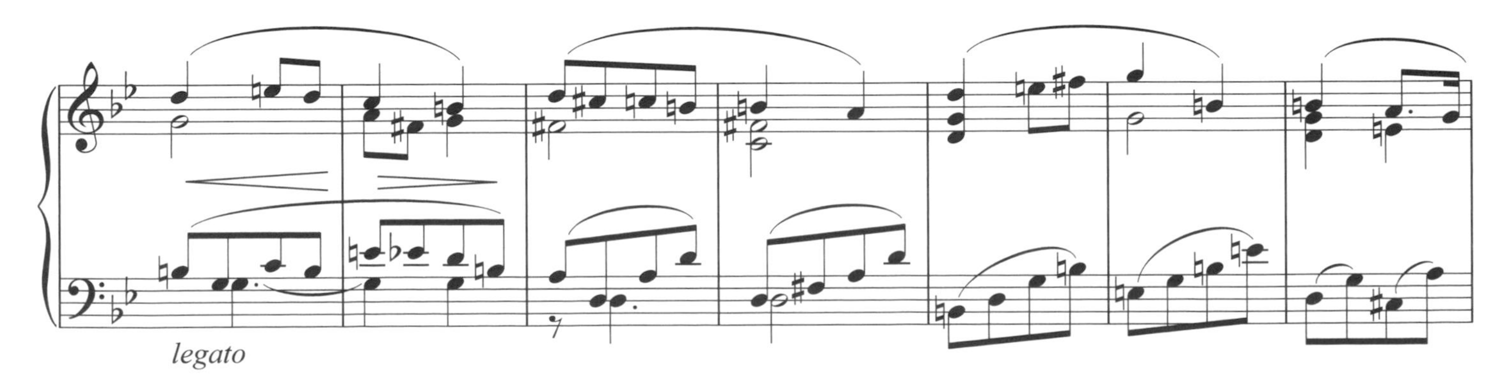

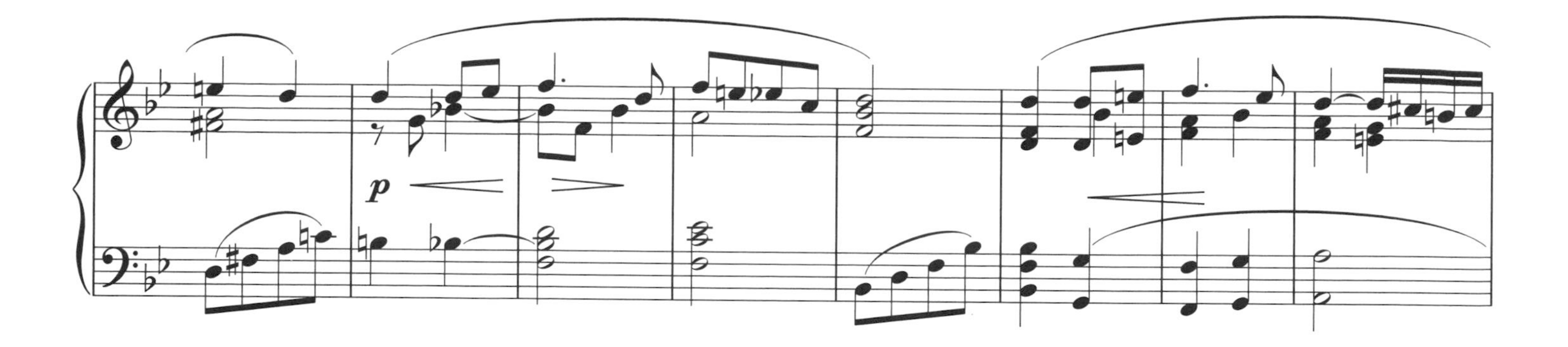
p

p
ten.

p dolce

pp

# BARCAROLLE
## (FROM 'THE TALES OF HOFFMANN')

Composed by Jacques Offenbach



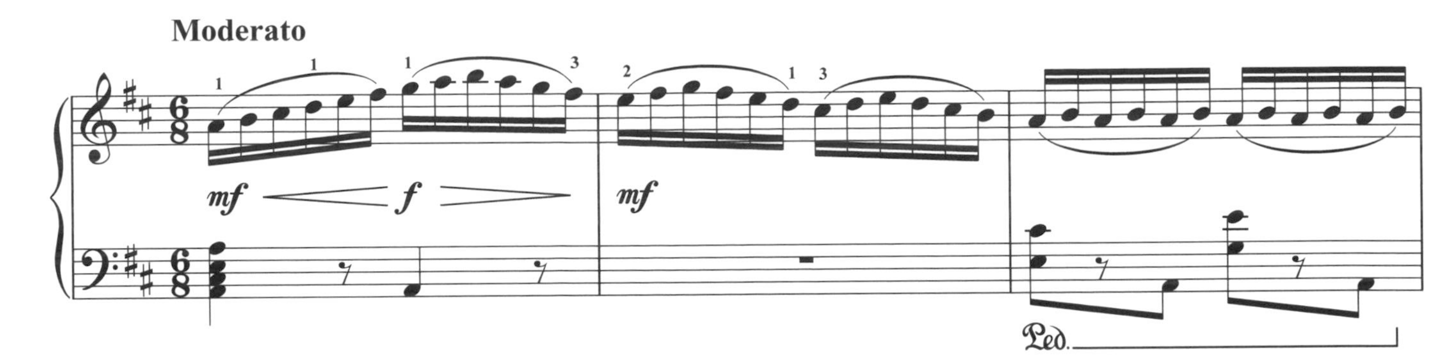

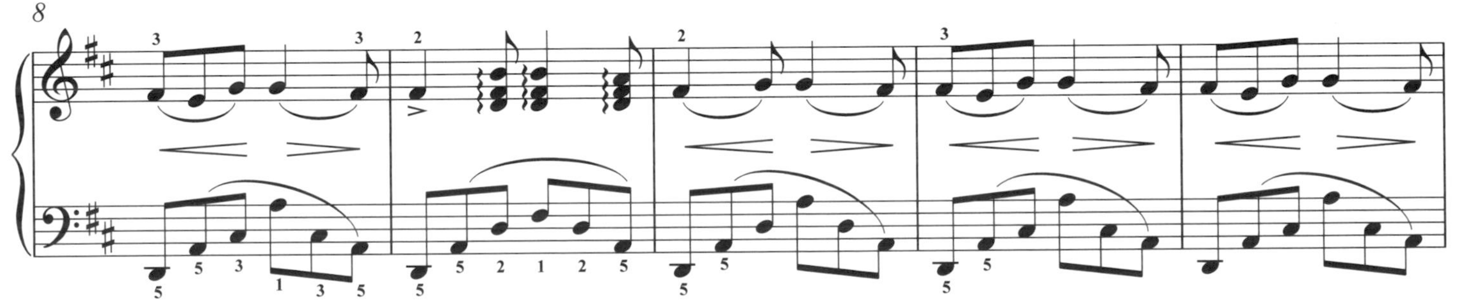

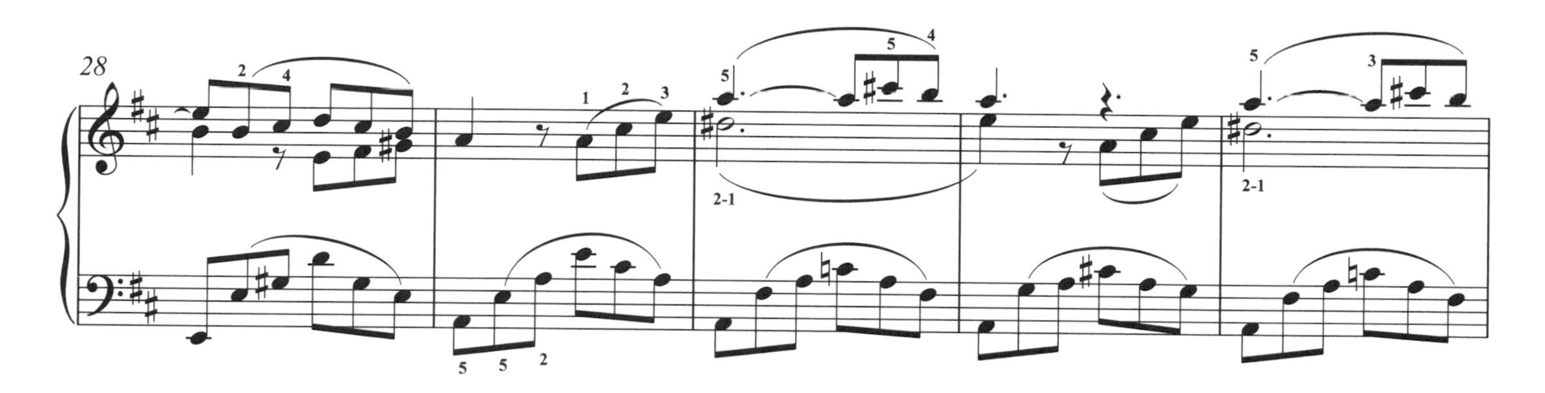

pp bien marque le chant
Ped.
simile

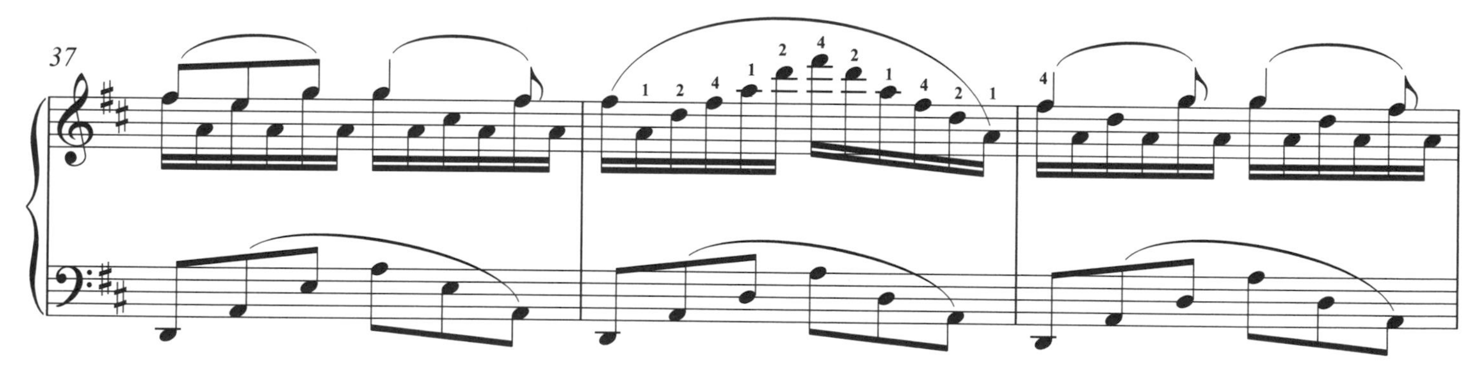

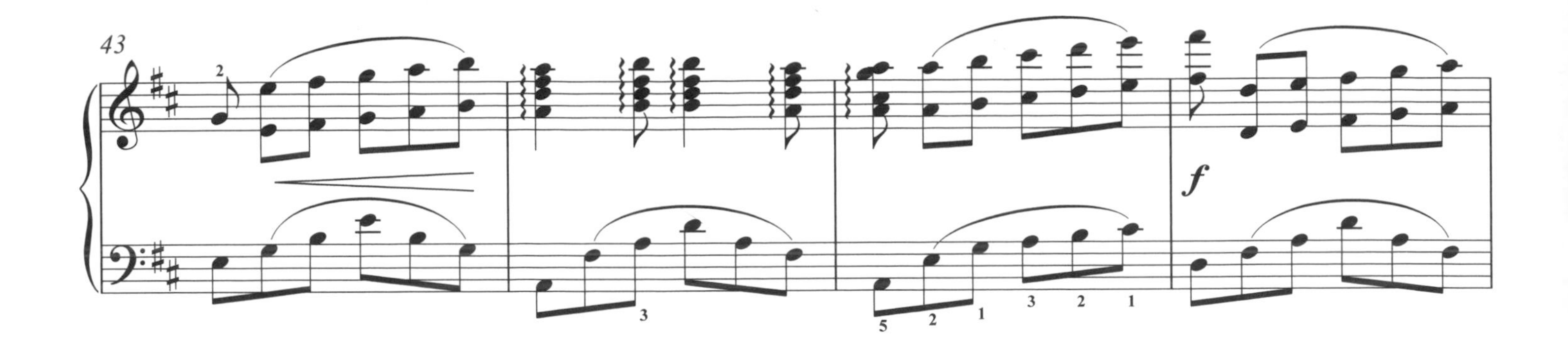
43
f

47
p

51
sempre più dolce

55
morendo

59
pp
ppp

# Chorus Of The Hebrew Slaves

## ('Va pensiero' from 'Nabucco')

Composed by Giuseppe Verdi

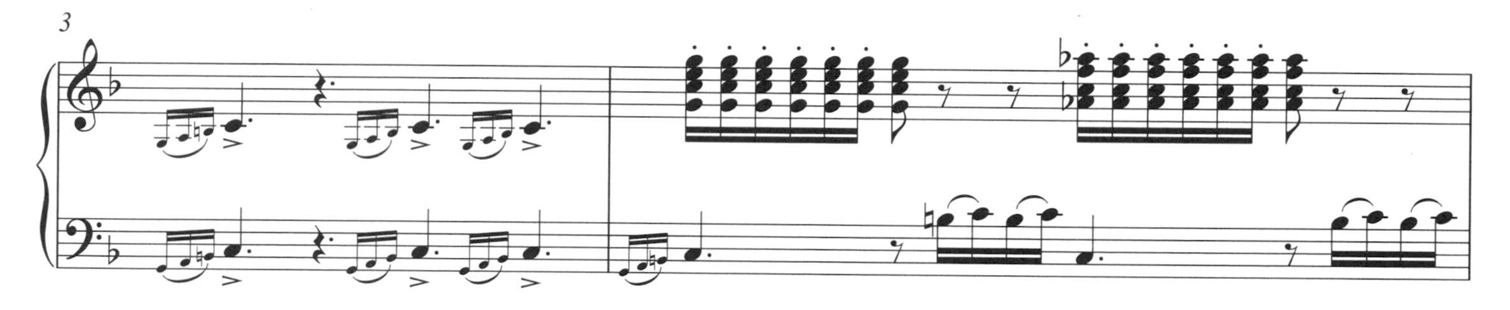

12
cantabile (poco meno mosso)
p

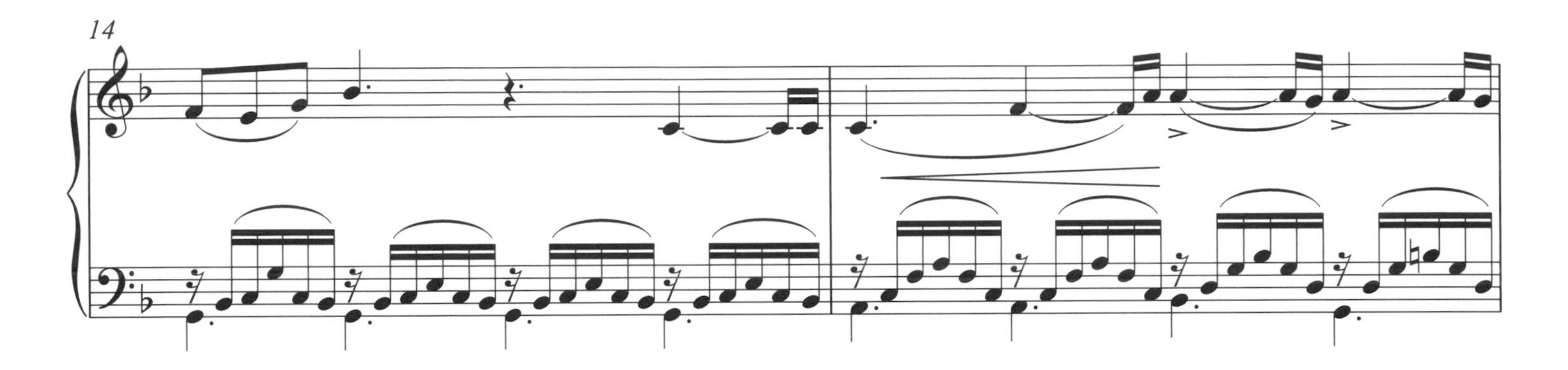
14

16

18

20

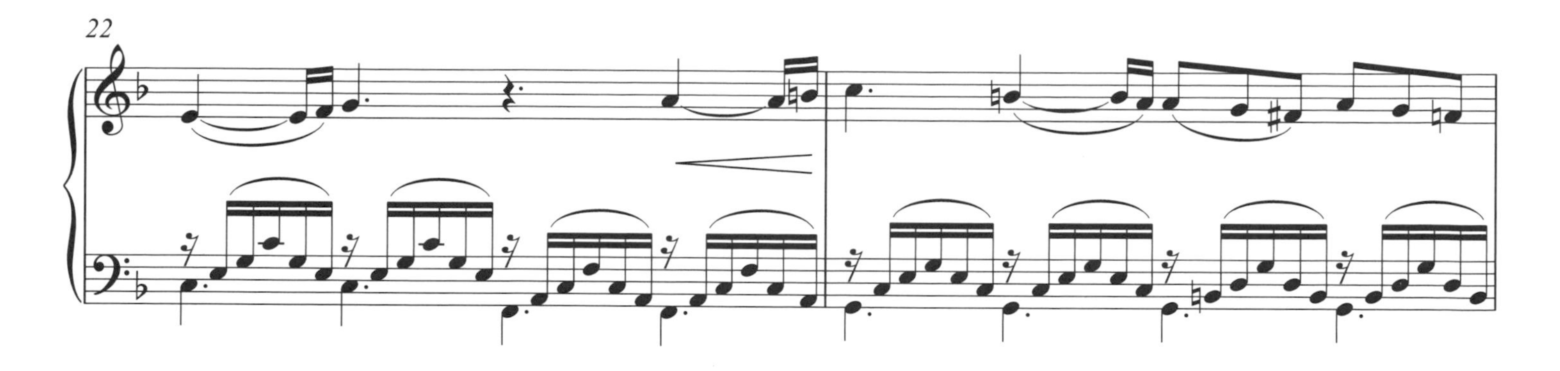
22

24

26

28
ff marc.

30
pp

32
ff marc.

34
p
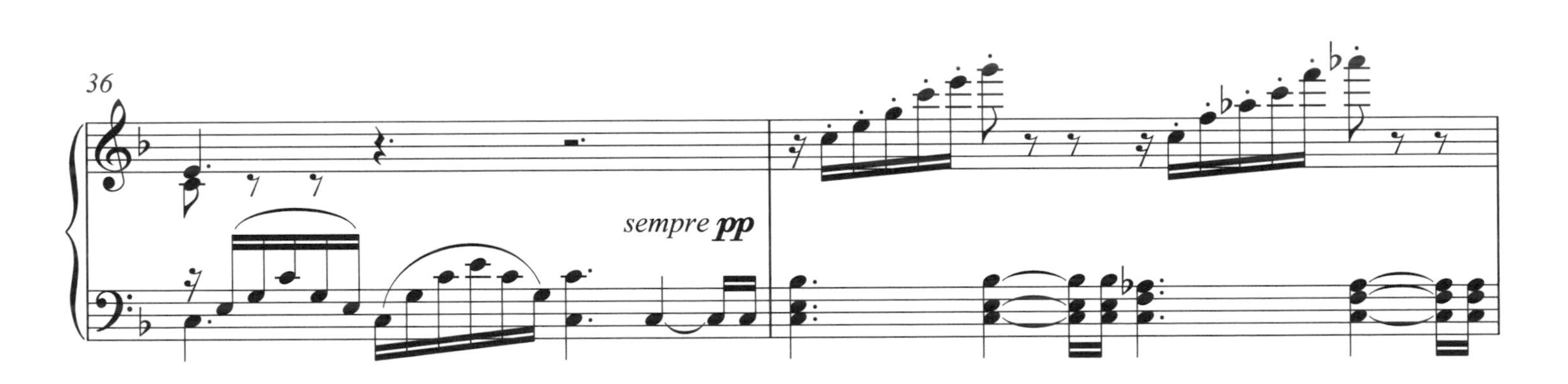
36
sempre pp

38

40
cresc.

41

43

45

47
pp

49
ppp

# Casta diva
## (from 'Norma')

Composed by Vincenzo Bellini

Arranged by Simon Lesley



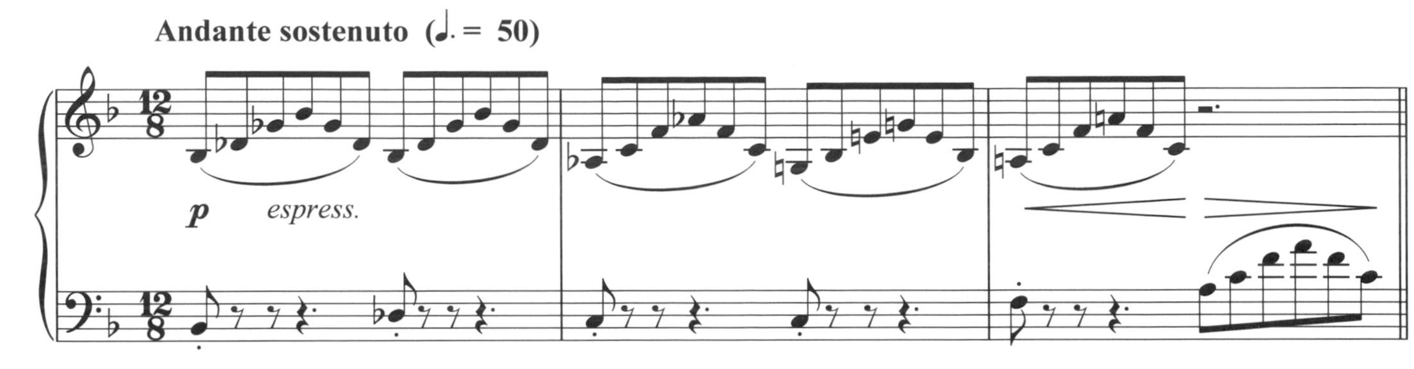


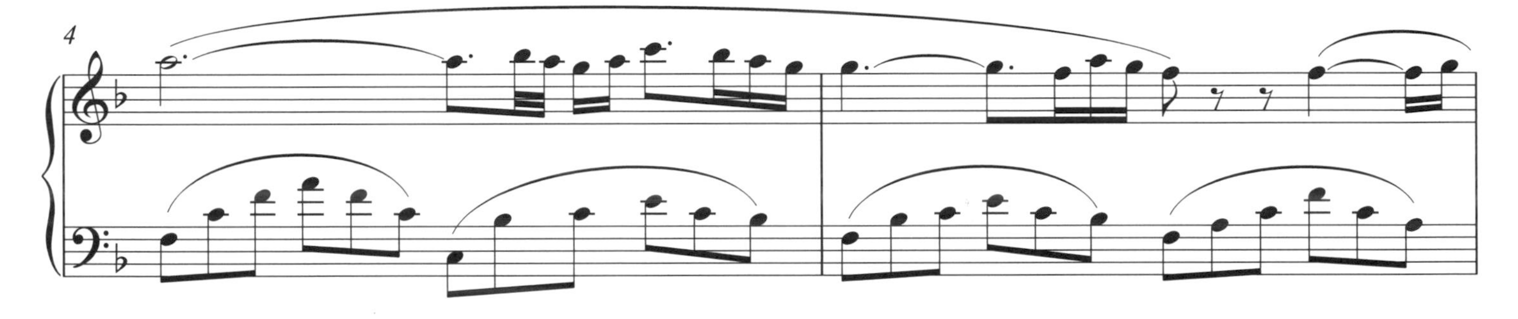


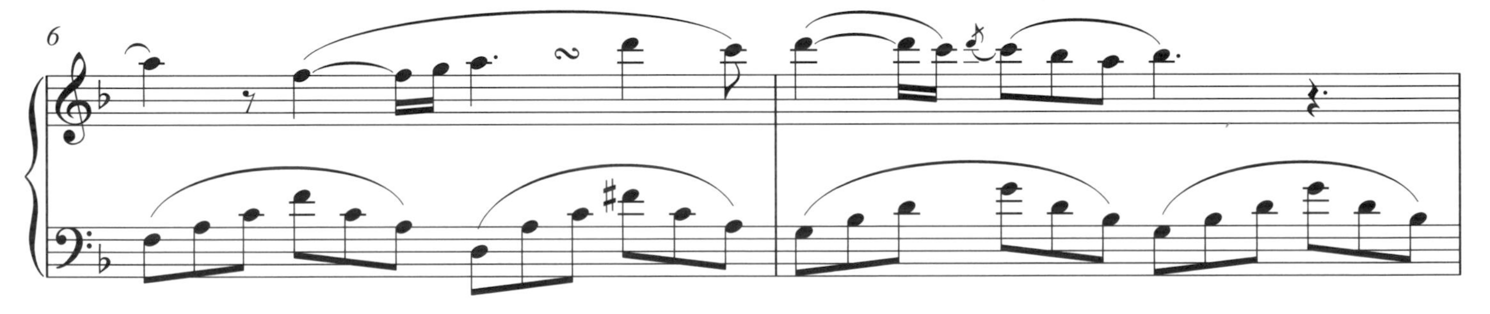


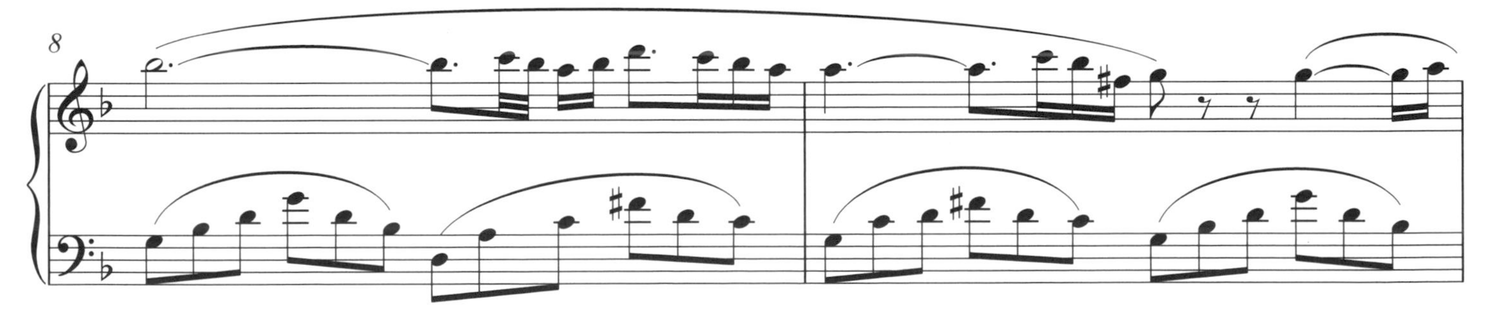


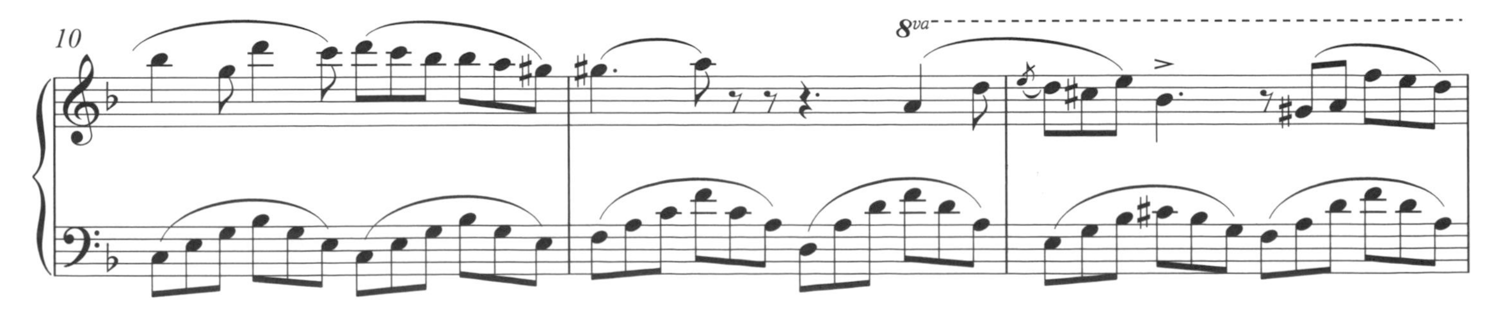

(8)
13
cresc.

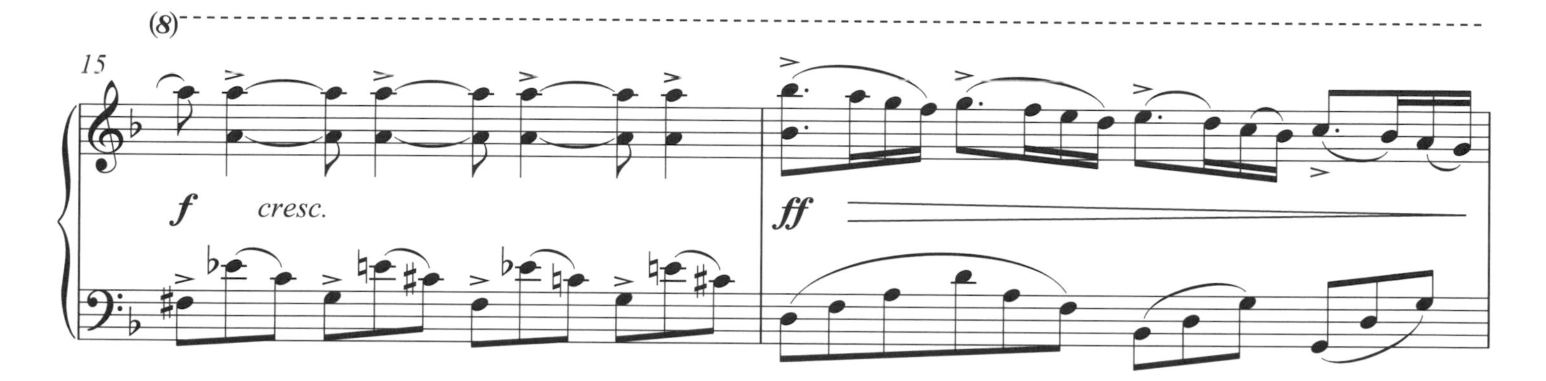
(8)
15
f
cresc.
ff

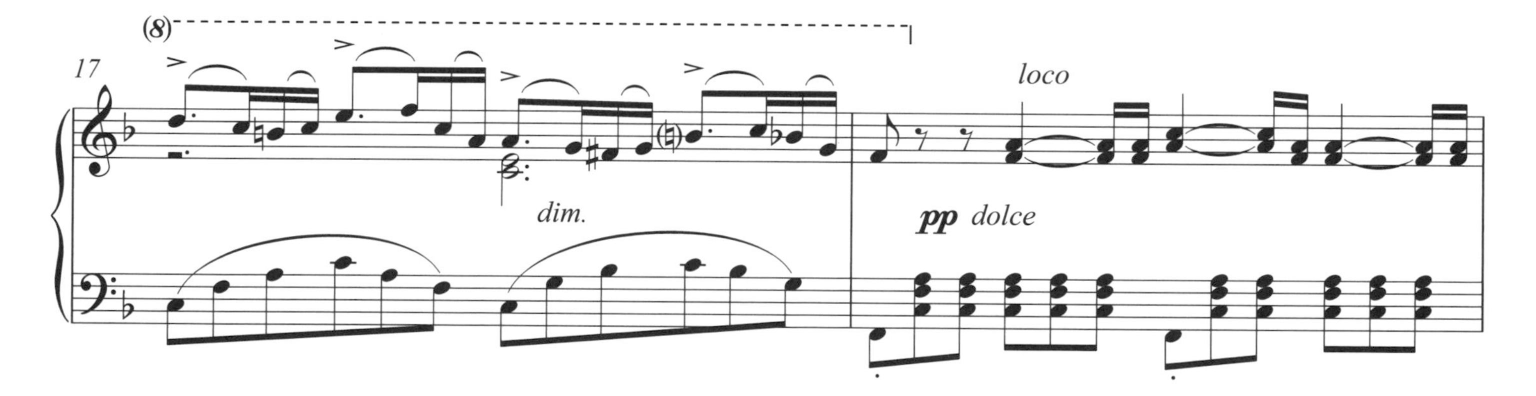
(8)
17
dim.
loco
pp dolce

19

22

25

28
pp
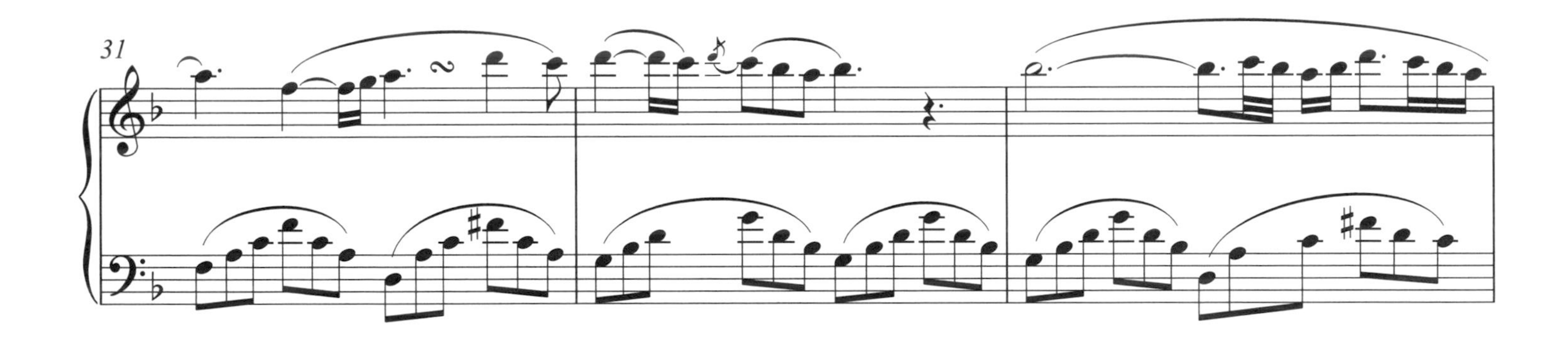
31

34

36

38
cresc.

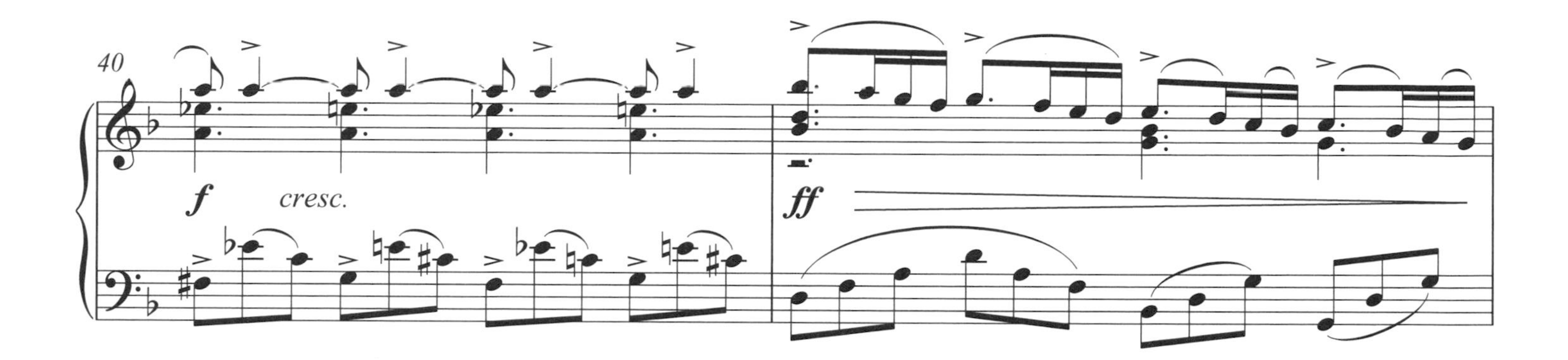
40
f
cresc.
ff

42
dim.
pp

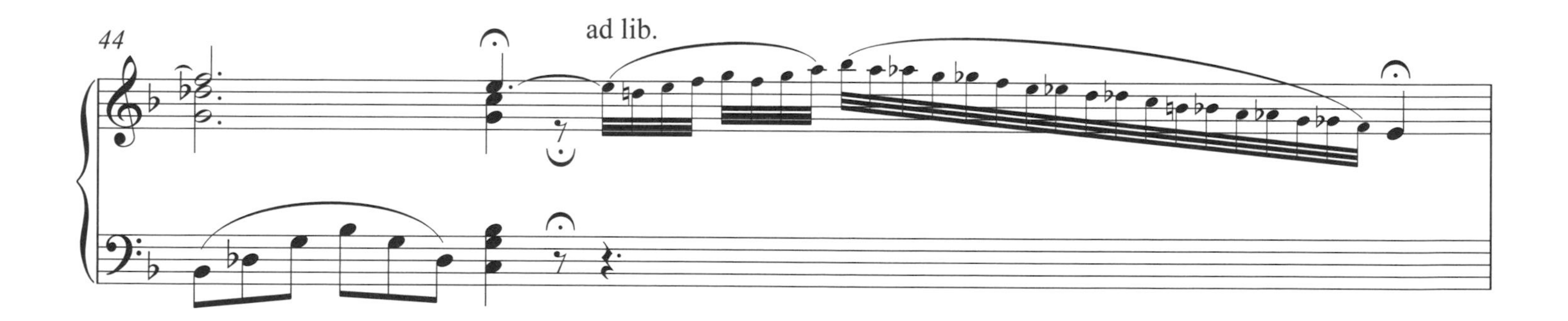
44
ad lib.

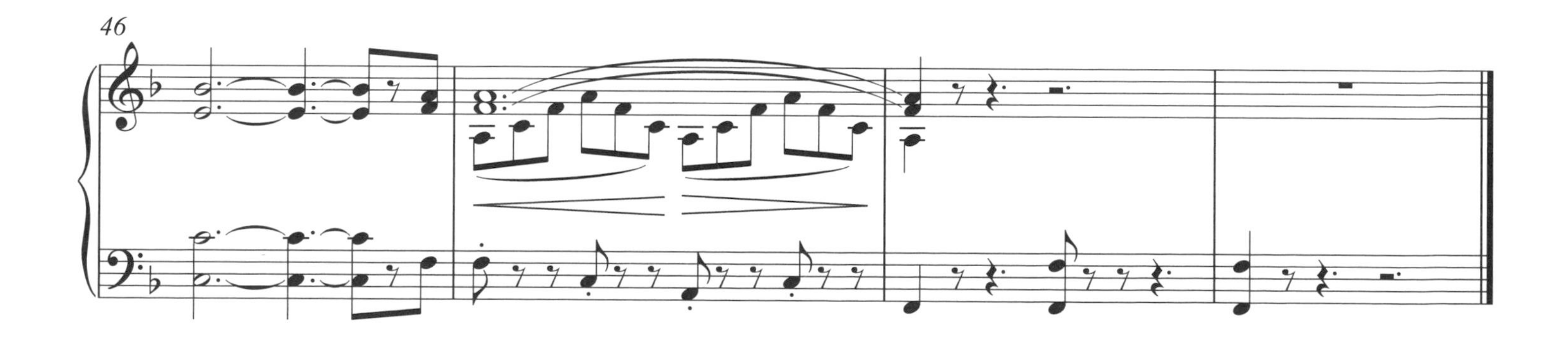
46

# Dance Of The Hours

(from 'La Gioconda')

Composed by Amilcare Ponchielli

Arranged by Jack Long

Meno mosso (♩ = c.132)
'THE HOURS OF NIGHT'
espress.
14

18

22
rit.
a tempo

26

**Allegro con brio**(♪ = c.168)
'DANCE OF ALL THE HOURS'

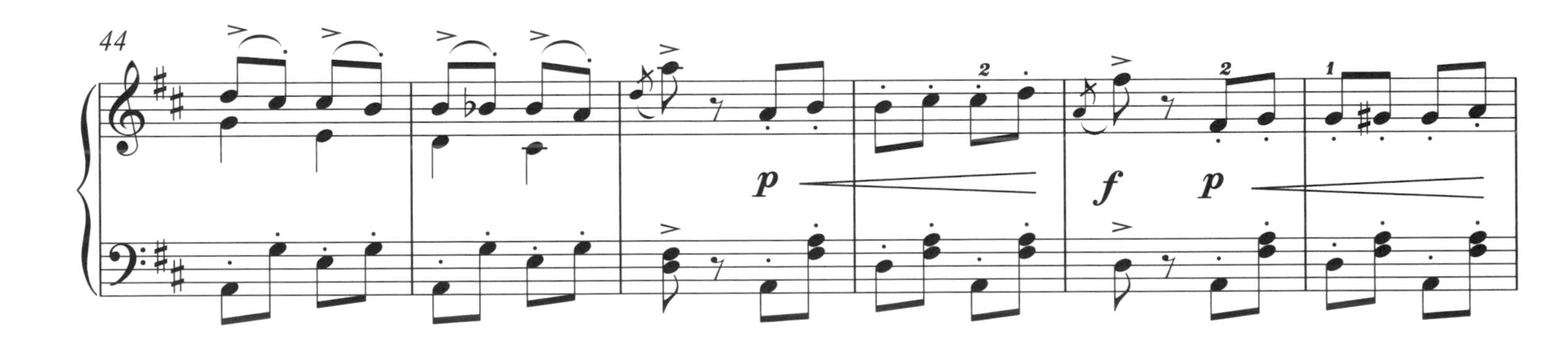

# Der Vogelfänger bin ich ja
## (from 'The Magic Flute')

Composed by Wolfgang Amadeus Mozart

Arranged by Jack Long



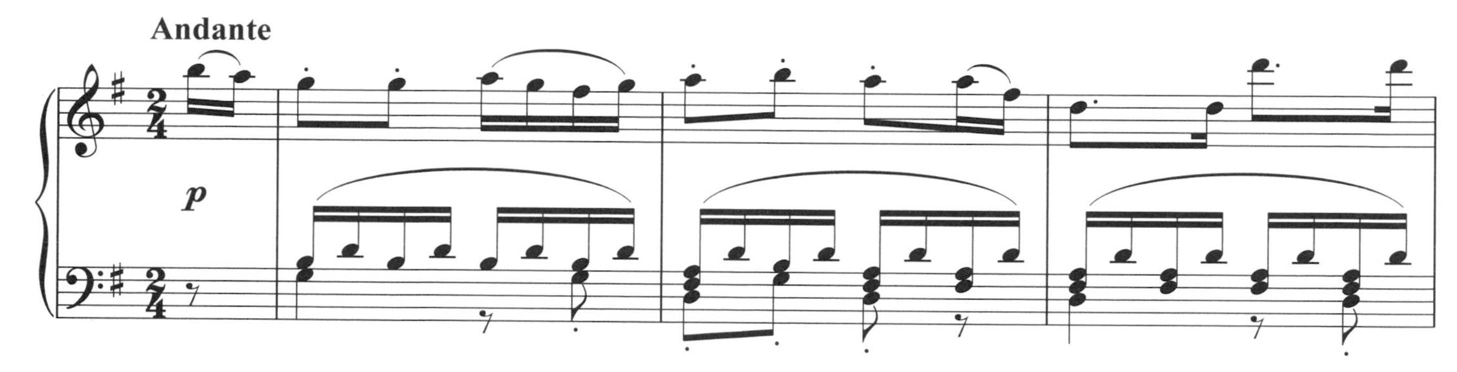

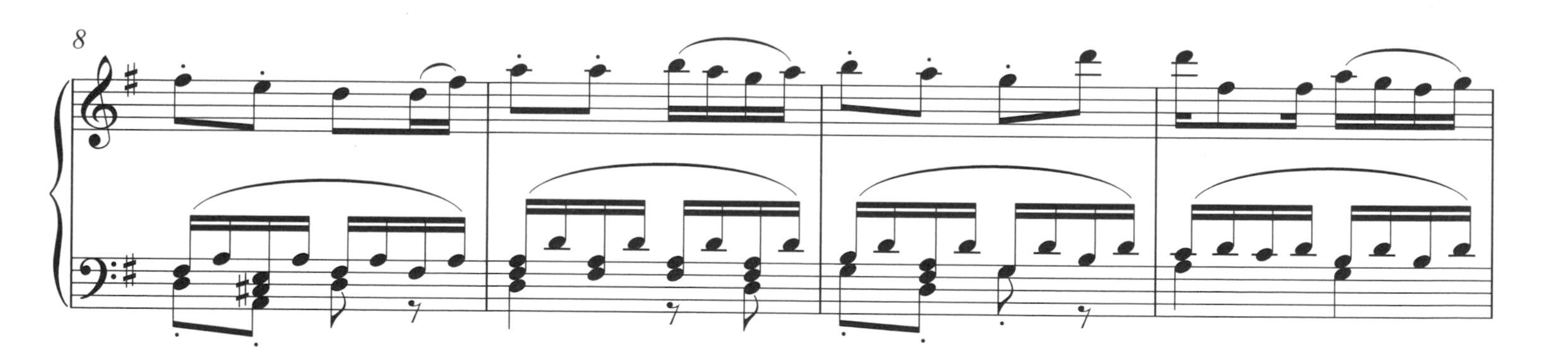


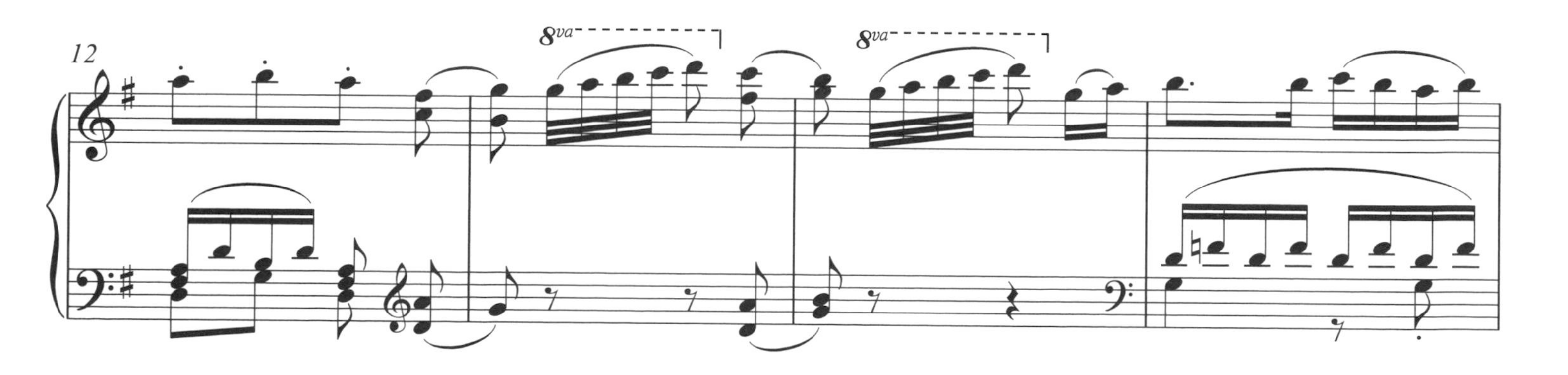

16
cresc.

20
f
8va

23
(8)
8va
p
f
p

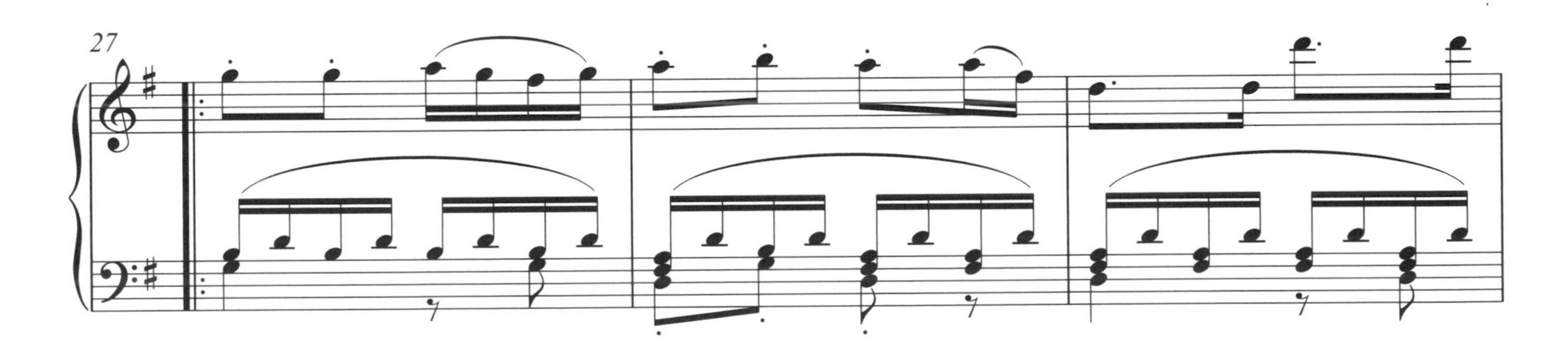
27

30

34
f
p

38
8va

42
8va

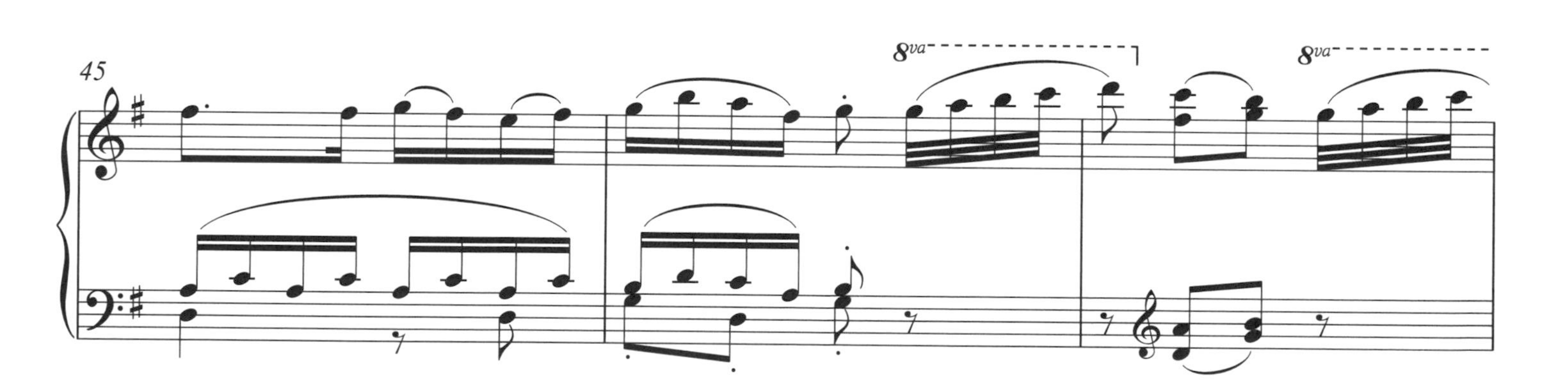
45
8va
8va

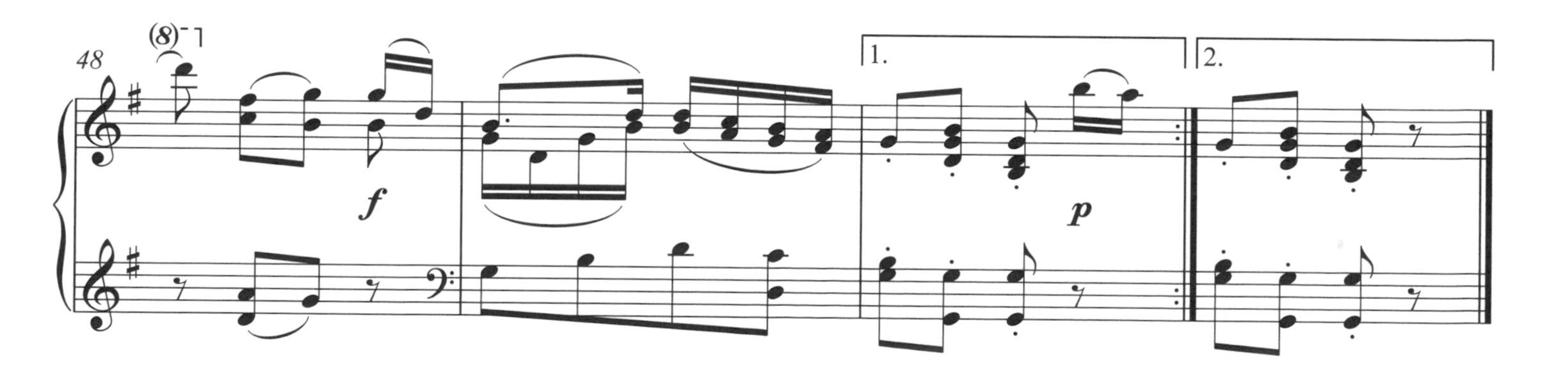
48
(8)
f
1.
2.
p

# E lucevan le stelle
## (from 'Tosca')

Composed by Giacomo Puccini

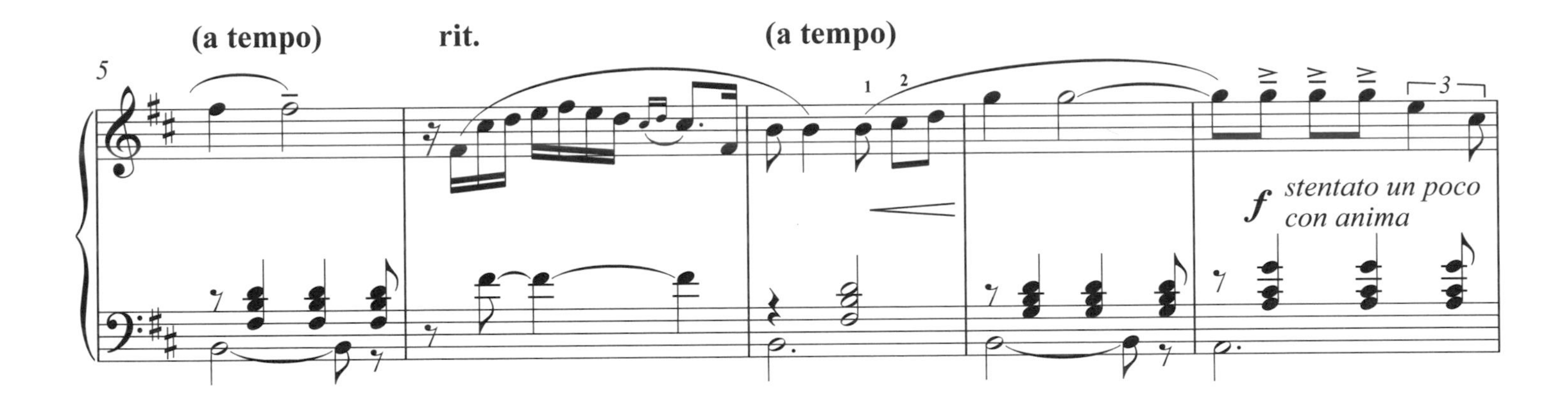


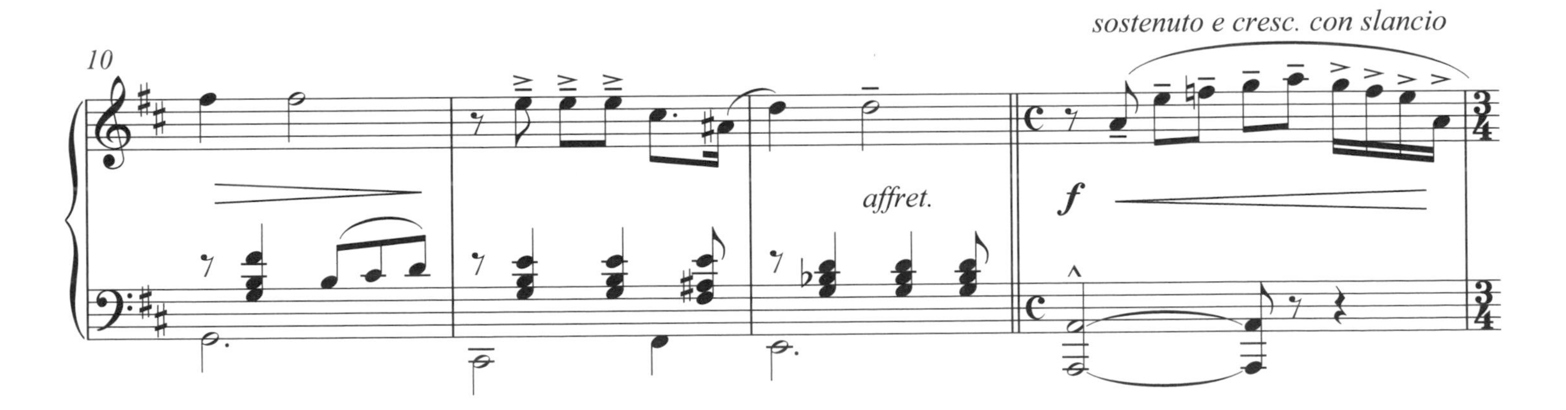

# AU FOND DU TEMPLE SAINT

## (DUET FROM 'THE PEARL FISHERS')

Composed by Georges Bizet

Arranged by Quentin Thomas

18

22
cresc. poco a poco

26
f
p

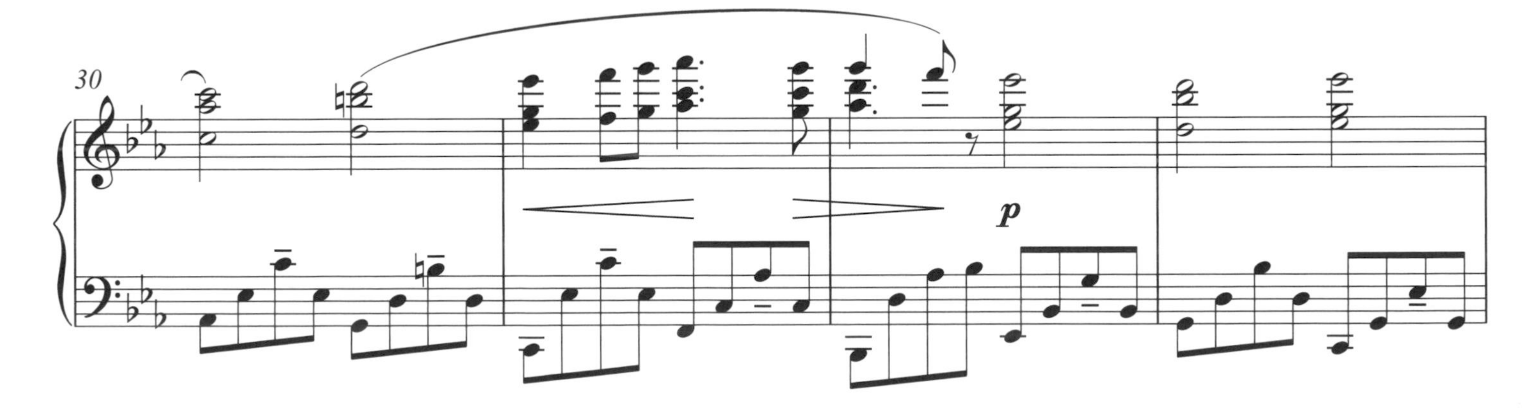
30
p

34
mf

38
f
ff

42

46
p

50

53
rit.
pp

# Flower Duet
## (from 'Lakmé')

Composed by Léo Delibes
Arranged by Jack Long

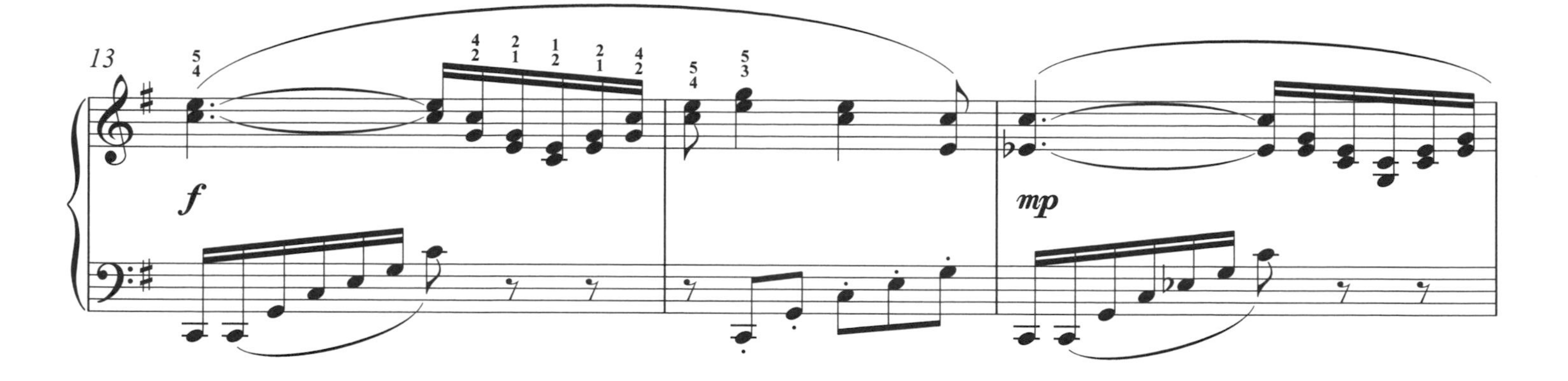
13
f
mp

16

poco rall.
a tempo
19
dim.
p
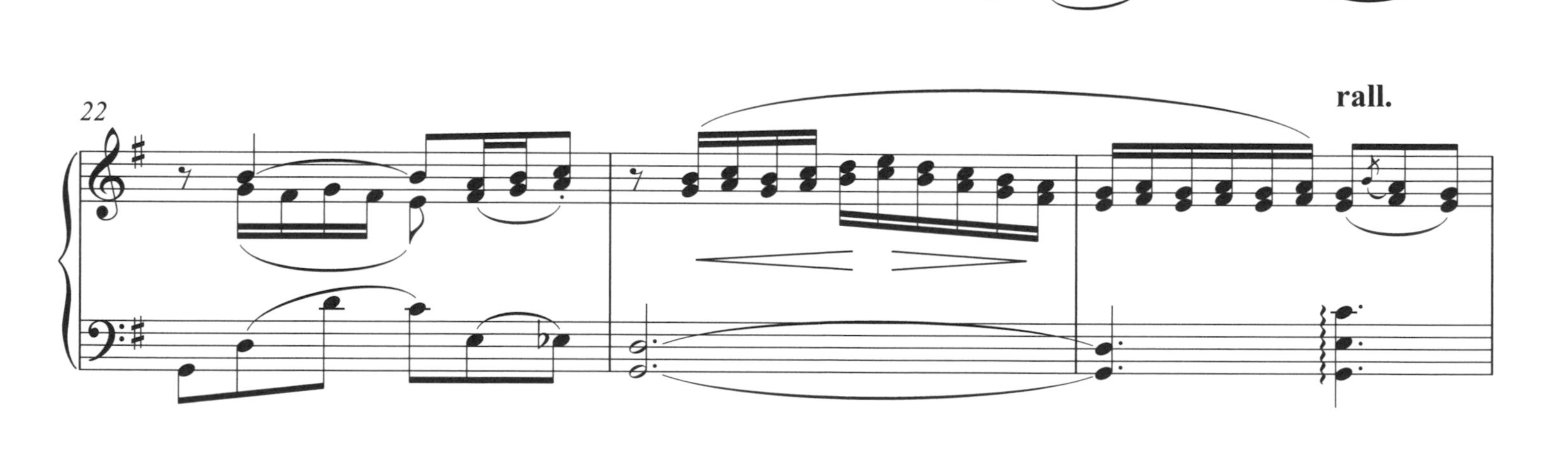
22
rall.
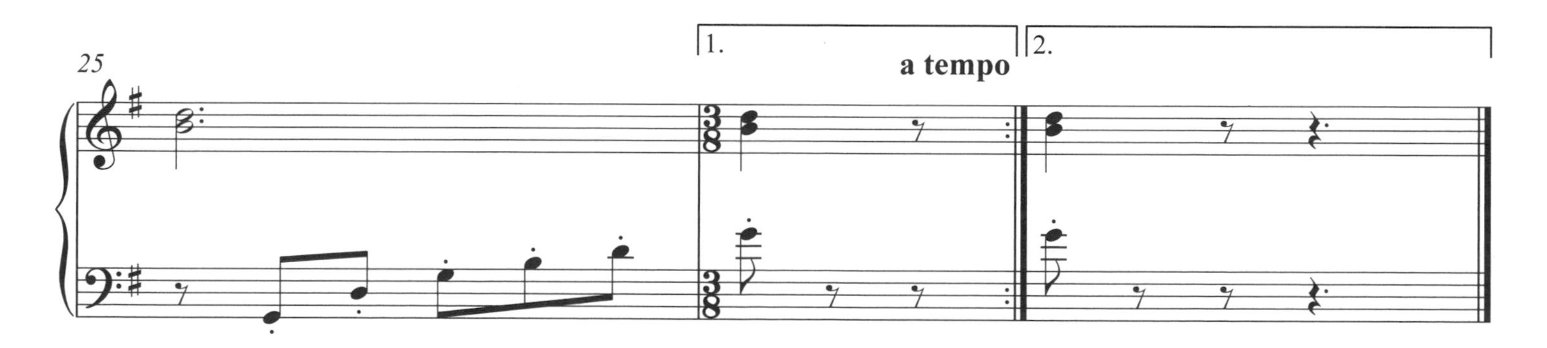
25
1.
2.
a tempo

# Grand March
## (from 'Aida')

Composed by Giuseppe Verdi

ff

ten.
ff

p

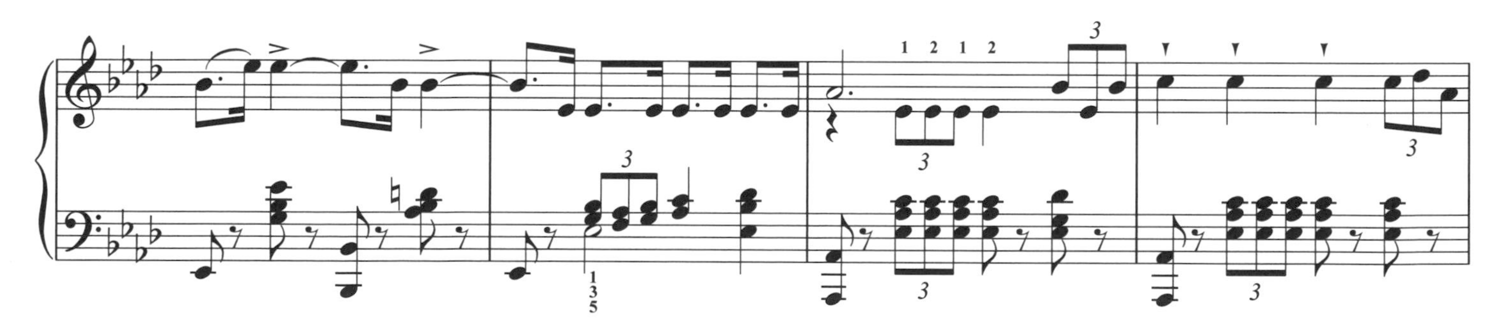

rit.
cresc.
ff

# Habanera

## ('L'amour est un oiseau rebelle' from 'Carmen')

Composed by Georges Bizet

Arranged by Jerry Lanning



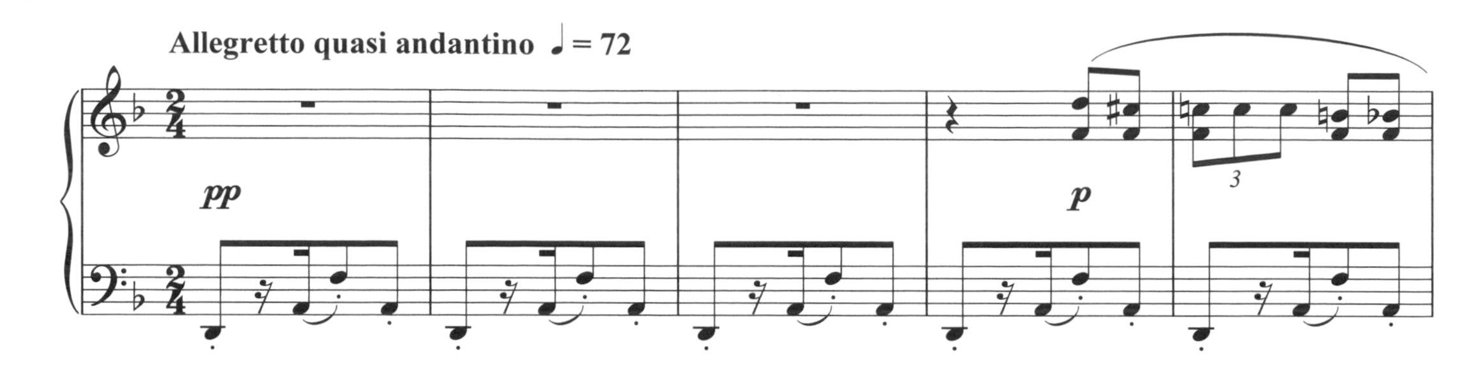


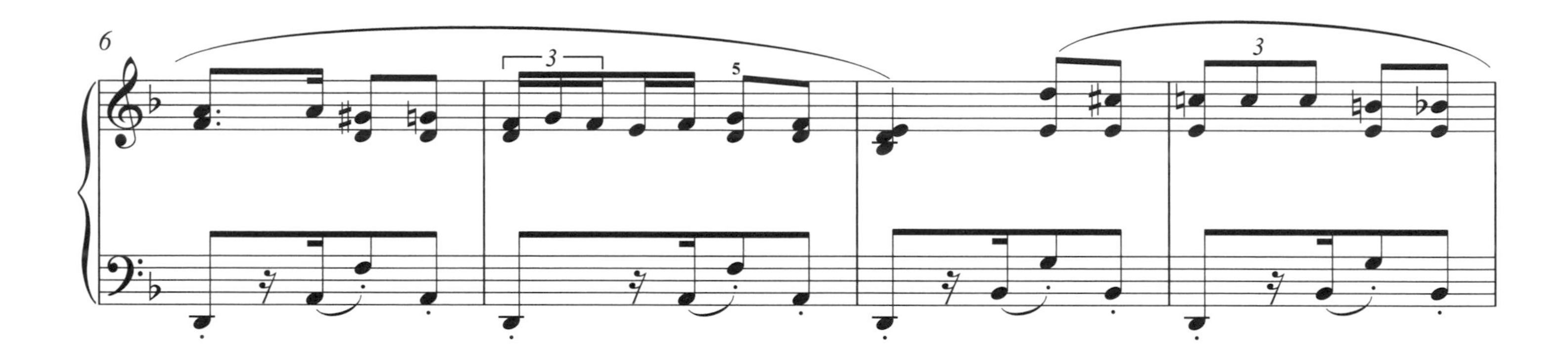


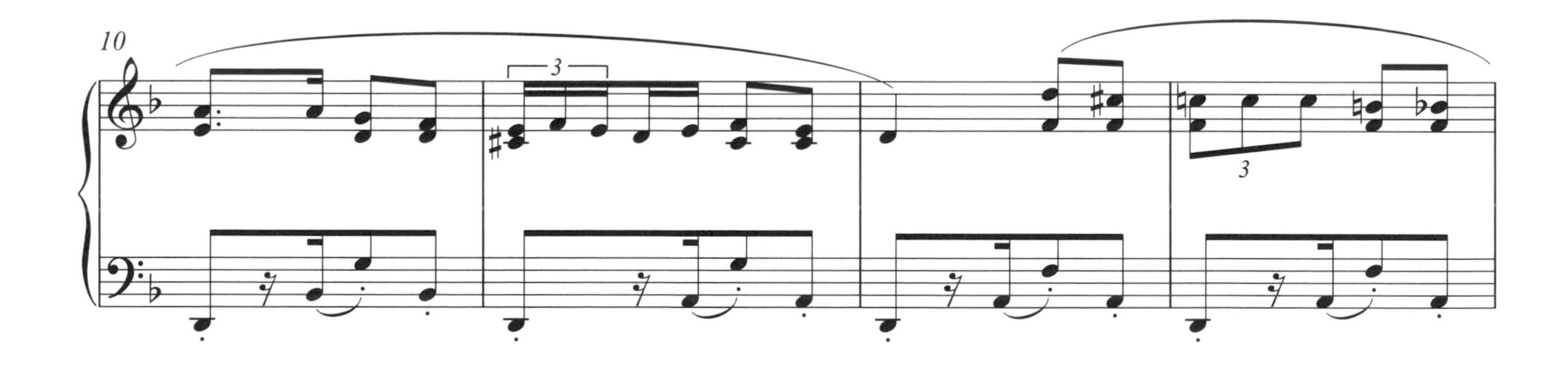


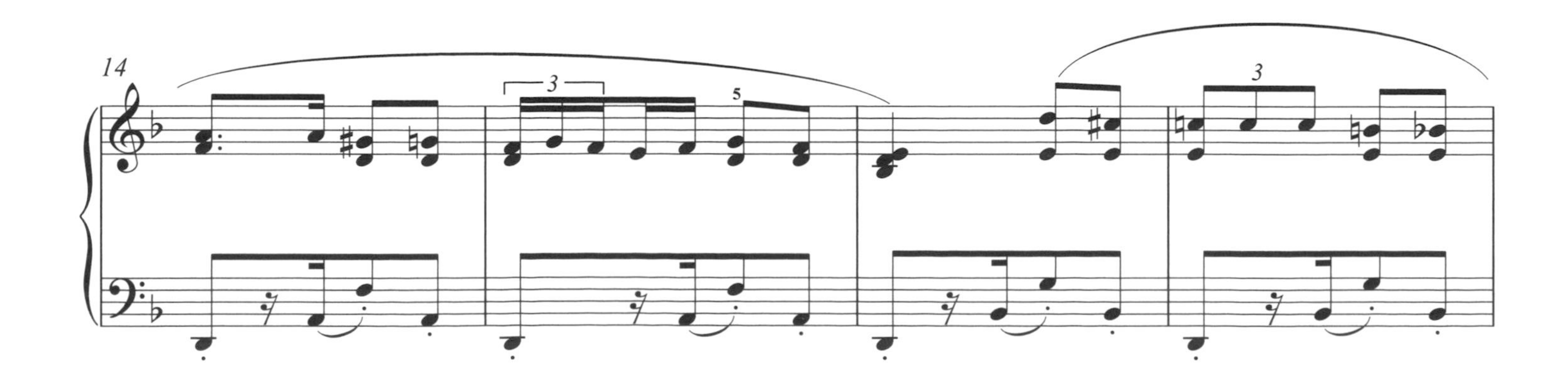

18
3
3


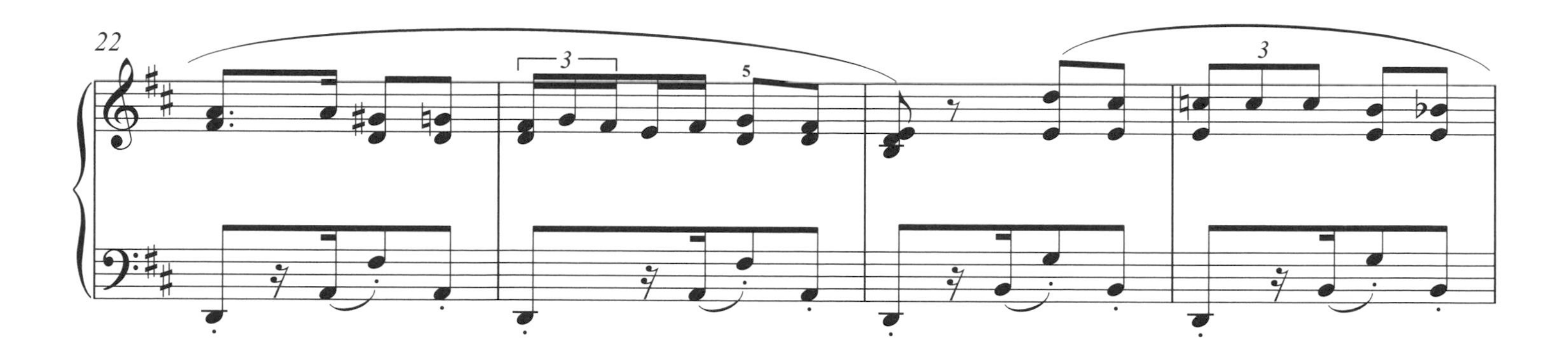
22
3
5
3


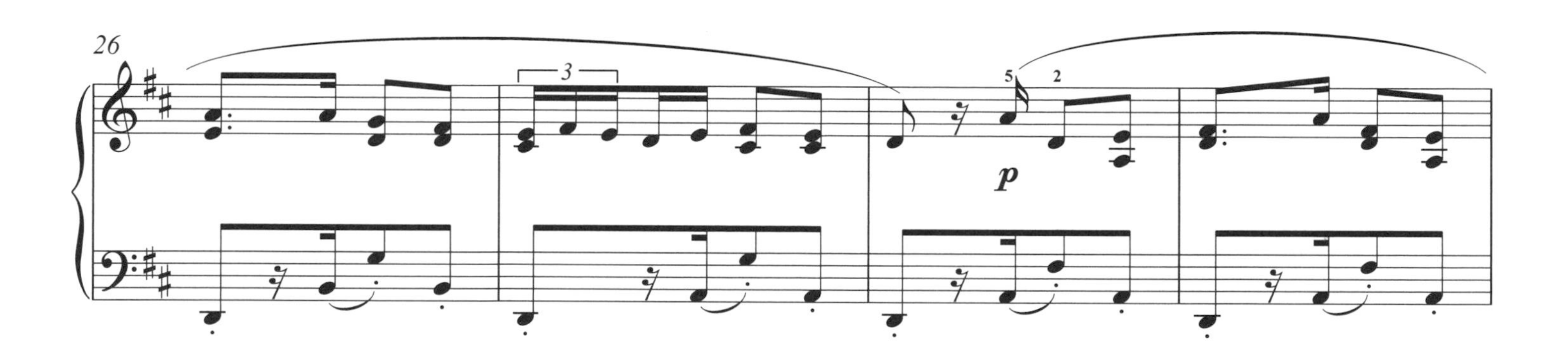
26
3
5
2
p


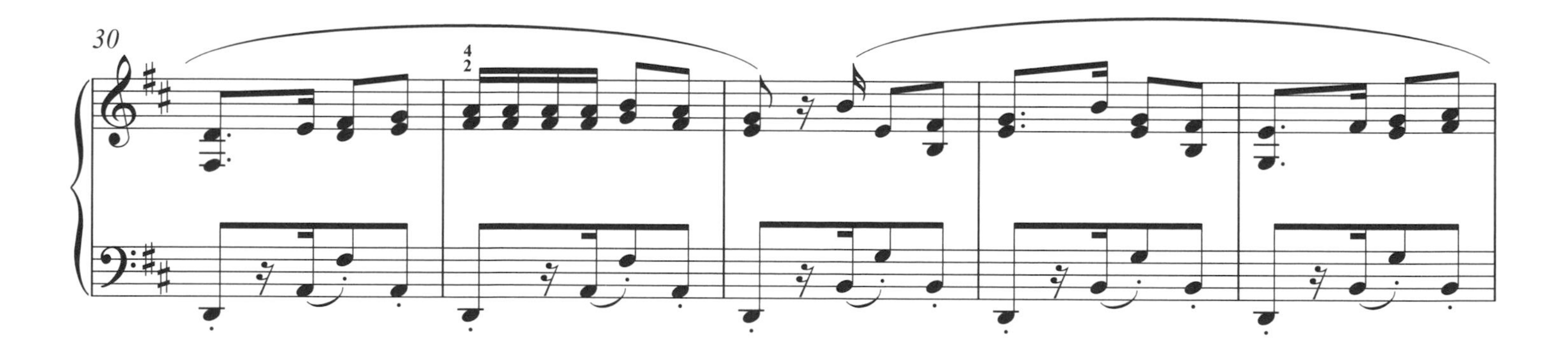
30
4
2

35
2
4
f
4
2
p

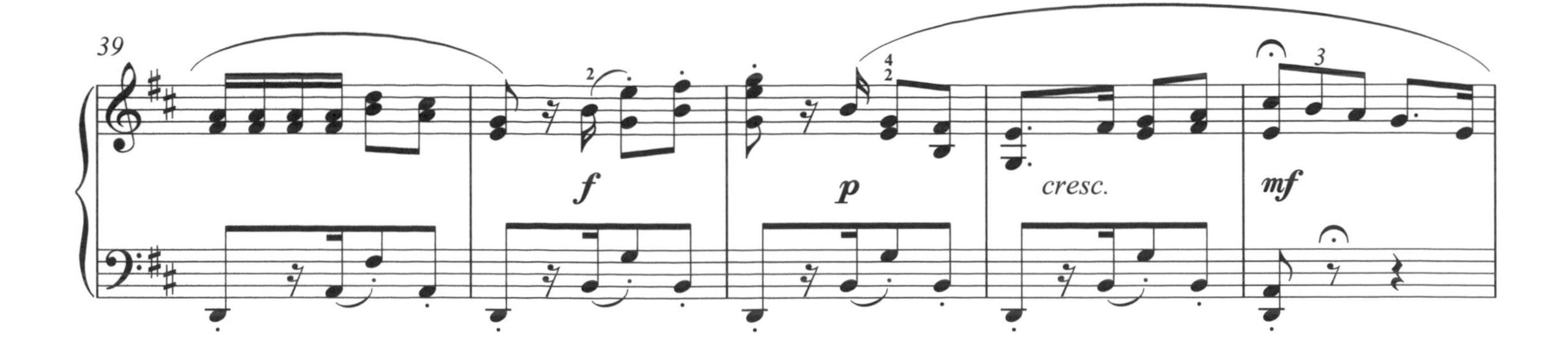
39
f
p
cresc.
mf

44

49
f

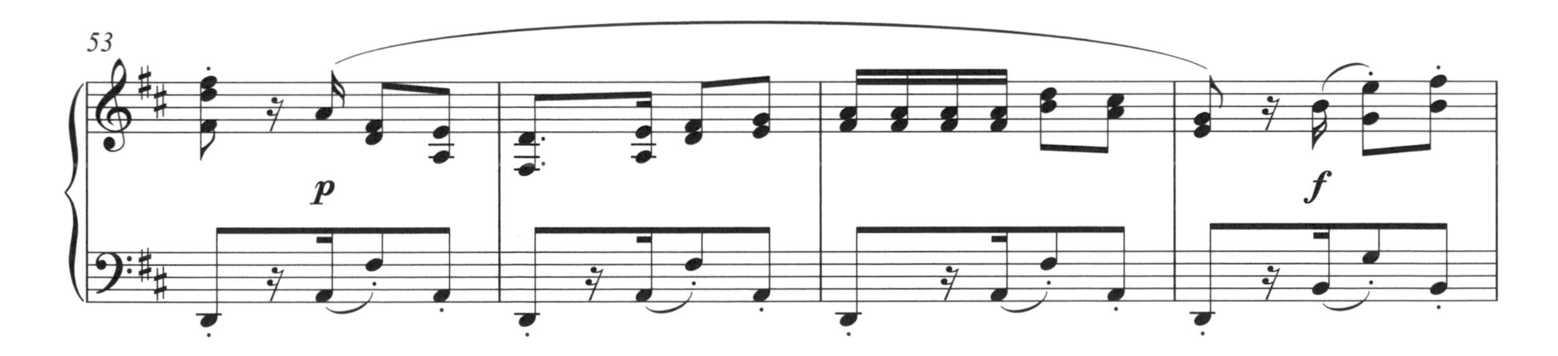
53
p
f

57
p
cresc.
f
ff

# Nessun dorma
## (from 'Turandot')

By Giacomo Puccini, Renato Simoni and Giuseppe Adami

Arranged by Jack Long

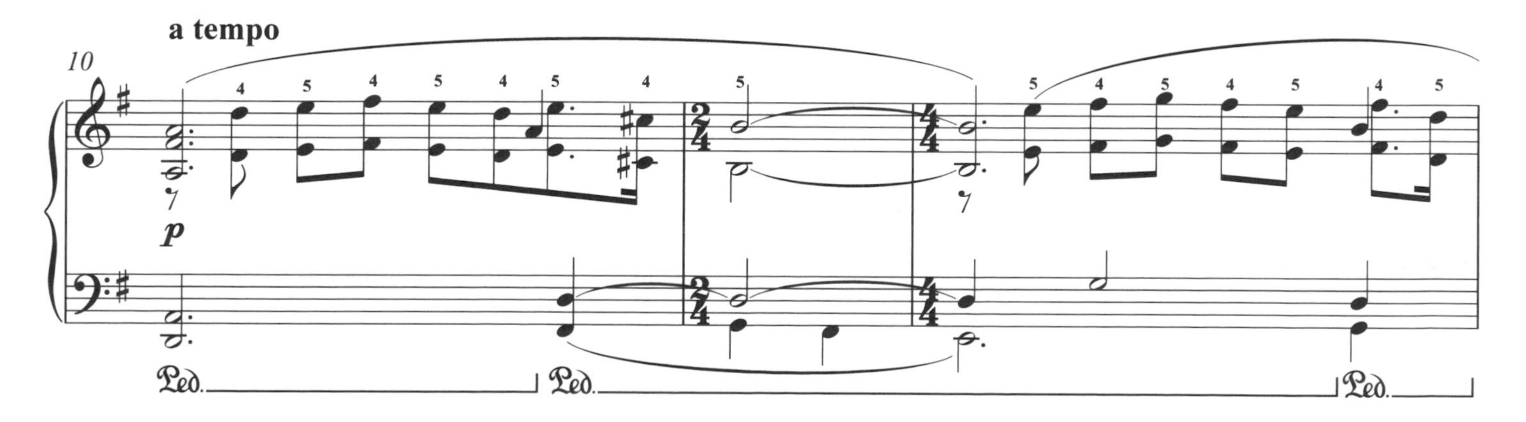

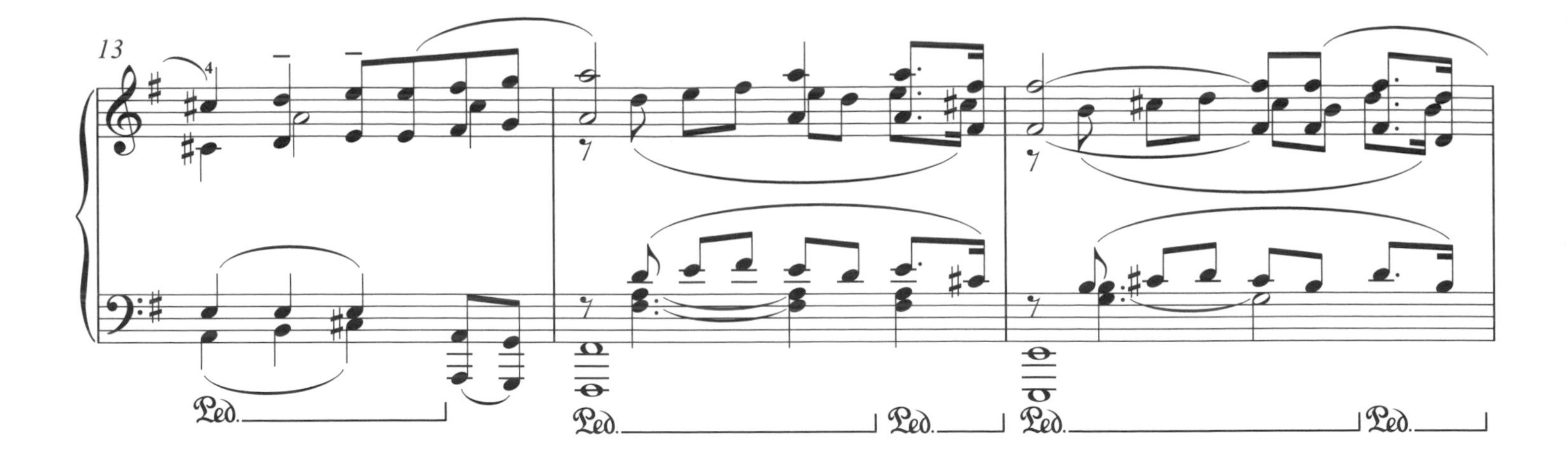
13
Ped.
Ped.
Ped.
Ped.
Ped.

16
Ped.
Ped.

19
rit.
Ped.
Ped.
Ped.

a tempo
22
ppp cresc.
Ped.
Ped.
Ped.

24
molto cresc.
Ped.
Ped.
Ped.

26
f
Ped.
Ped.
Ped.

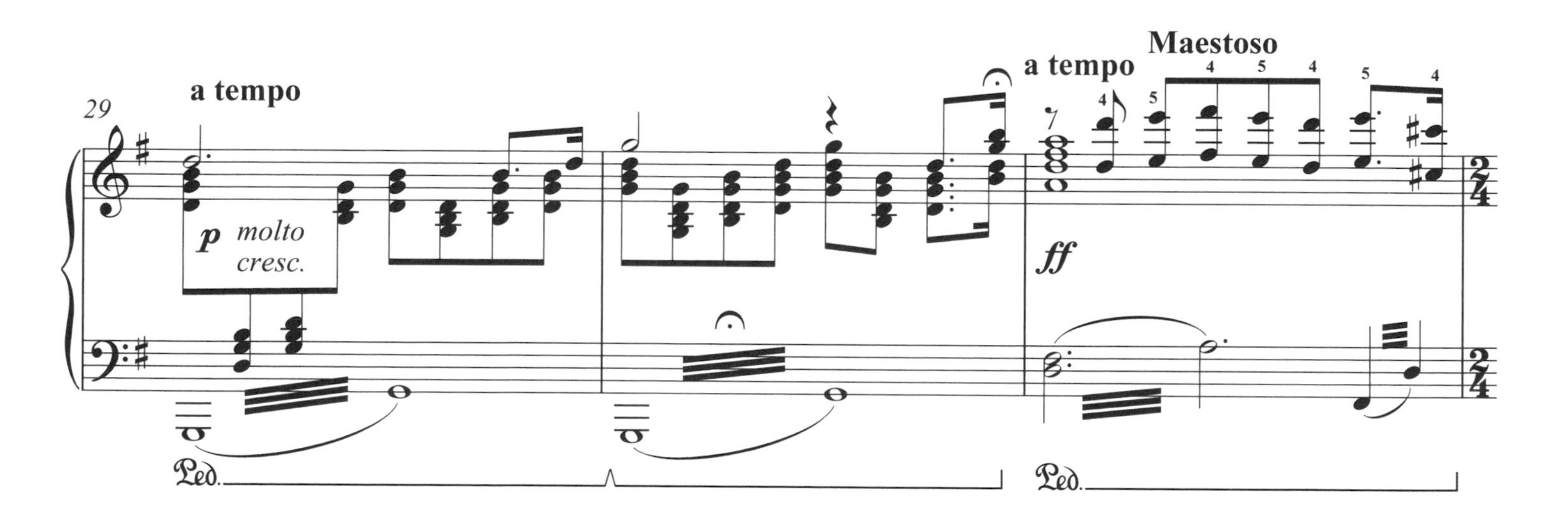
29
a tempo
p molto cresc.
a tempo
Maestoso
ff
Ped.
Ped.

32
rit.
8vb
Ped.
Ped.
Ped.
Ped.
Ped.
Ped.

# La donna è mobile
## (from 'Rigoletto')

Composed by Giuseppe Verdi
Arranged by Jerry Lanning



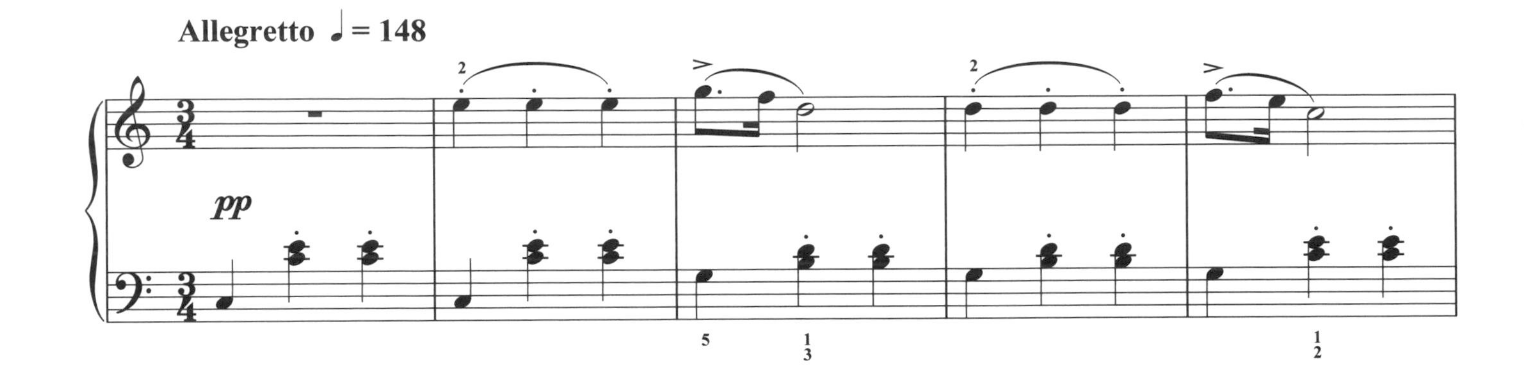

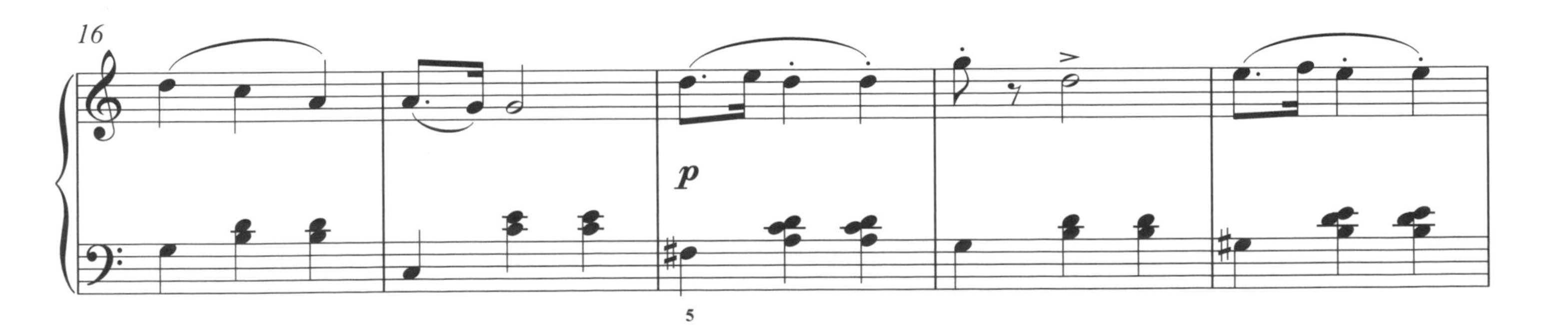

21
f
pp
3

26
3

30
cresc. poco a poco
3

34
Fine
f
grandioso

39
D.C. al Fine
p

# Largo
## ('Ombra mai fù' from 'Xerxes')

Composed by George Frideric Handel

p

mf


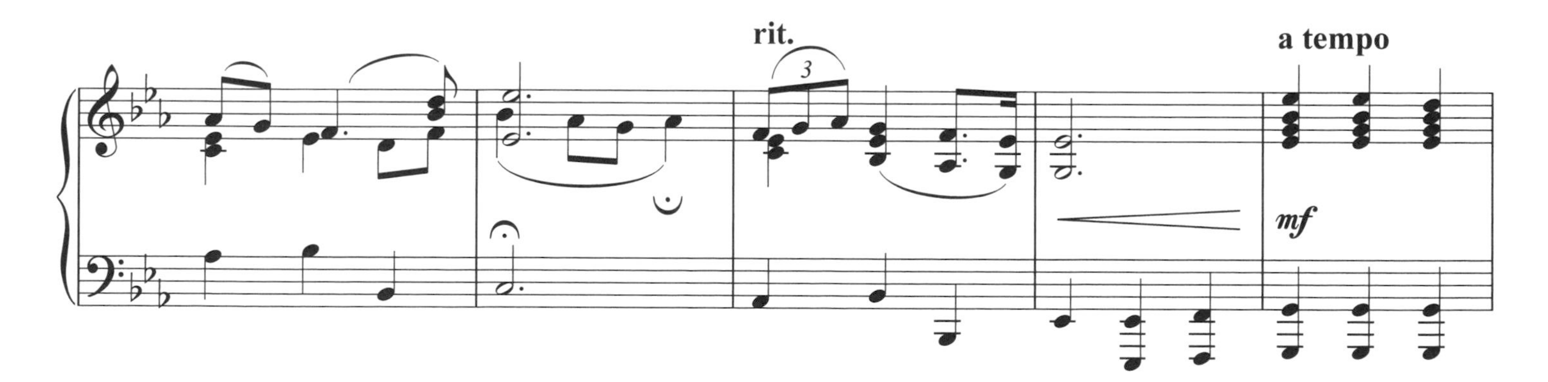

rit.
3
a tempo
mf

rit.
p

# Largo al factotum
## (from 'The Barber Of Seville')

Composed by Gioachino Rossini

Arranged by Jeremy Birchall

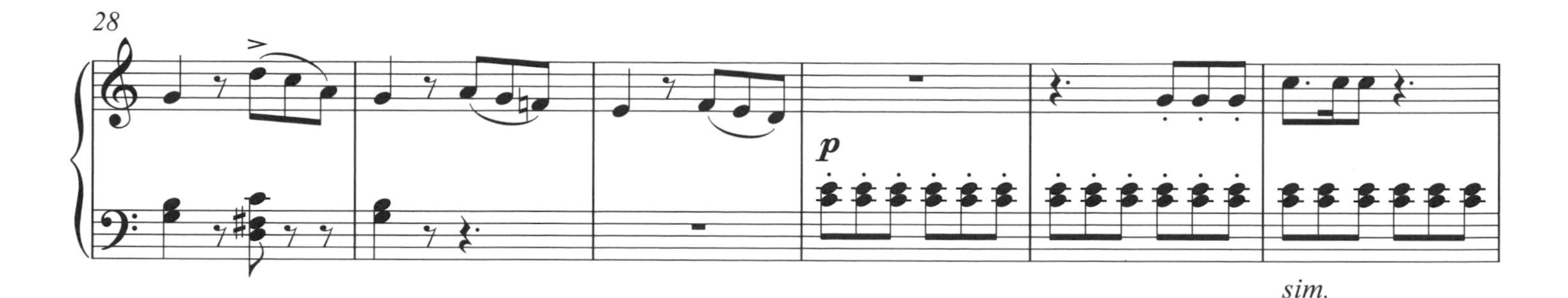
28
p
sim.

34

39

45

51
cresc.
f

57
f

63

68

73
p

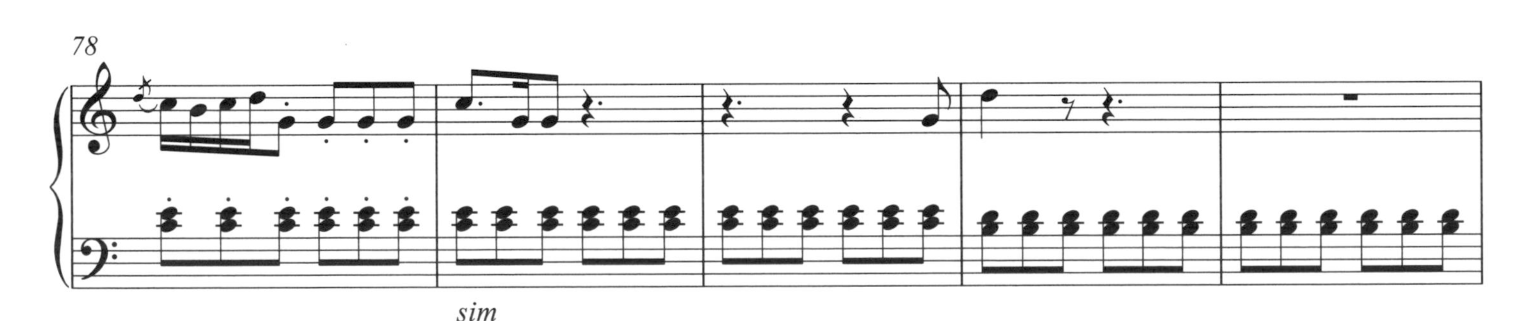
78
sim

83
cresc. sempre

88

93

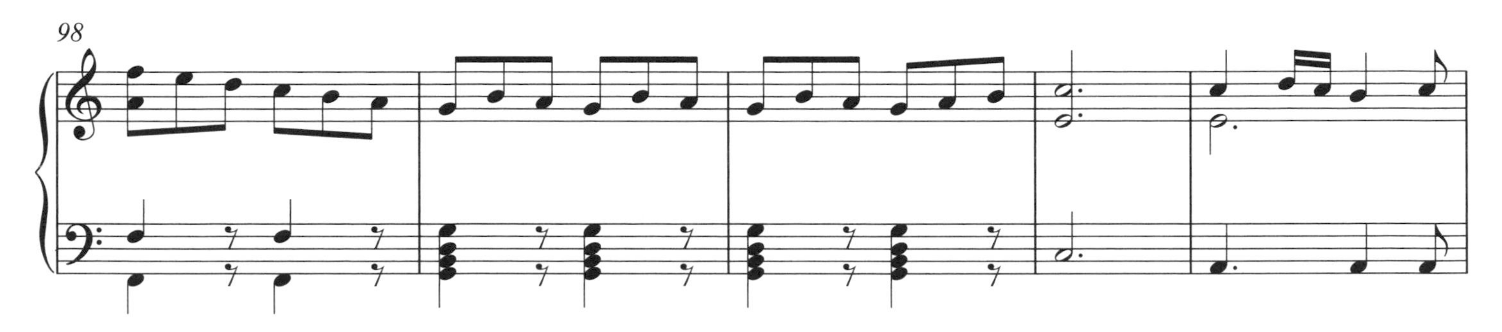
98

103

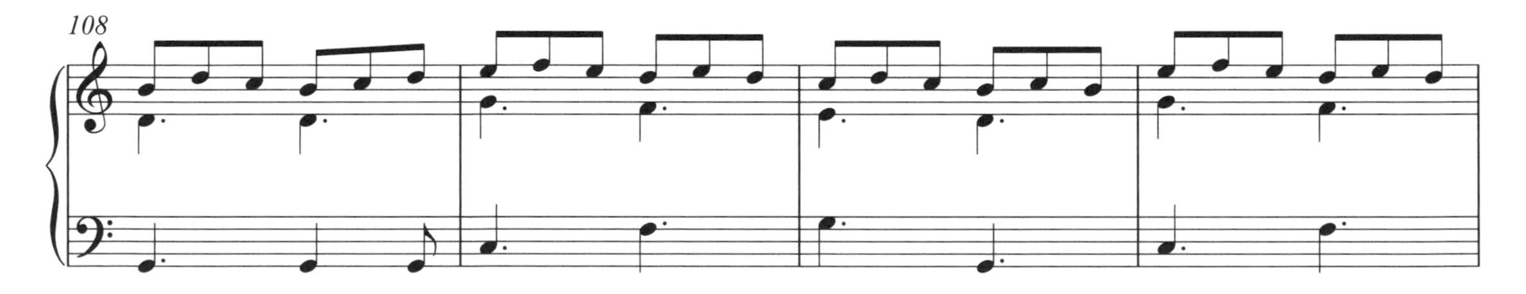
108

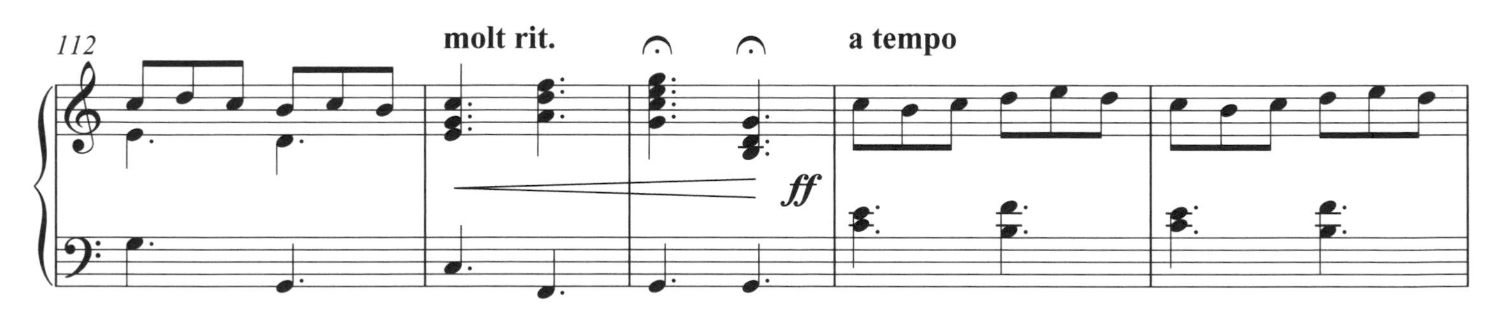
112
molt rit.
a tempo
ff

117

# Meditation

## (from 'Thaïs')

Composed by Jules Massenet

Arranged by Jerry Lanning

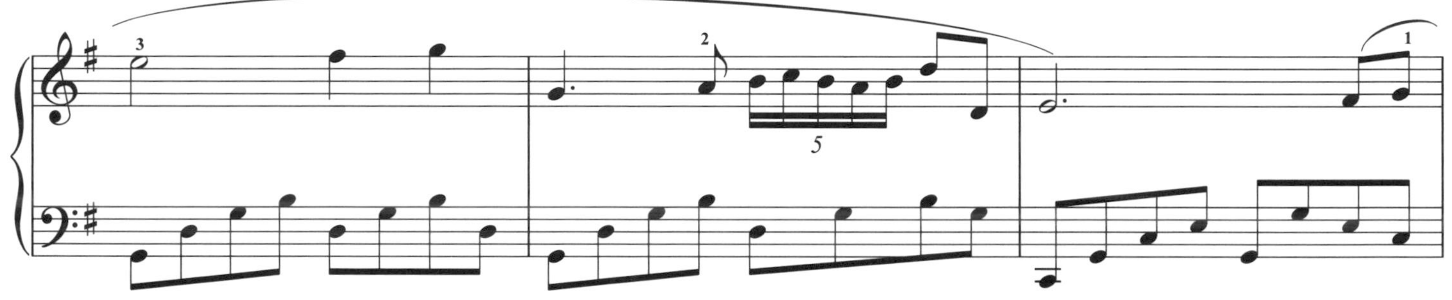

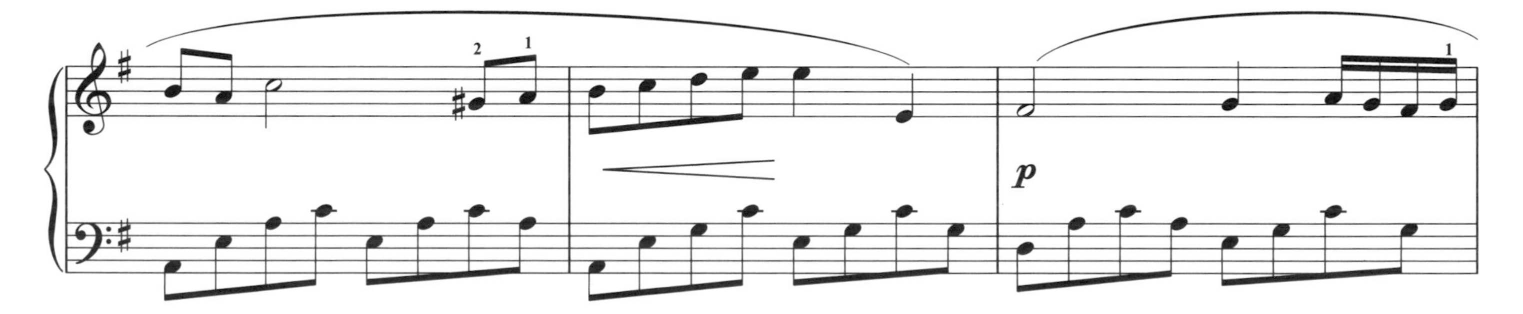


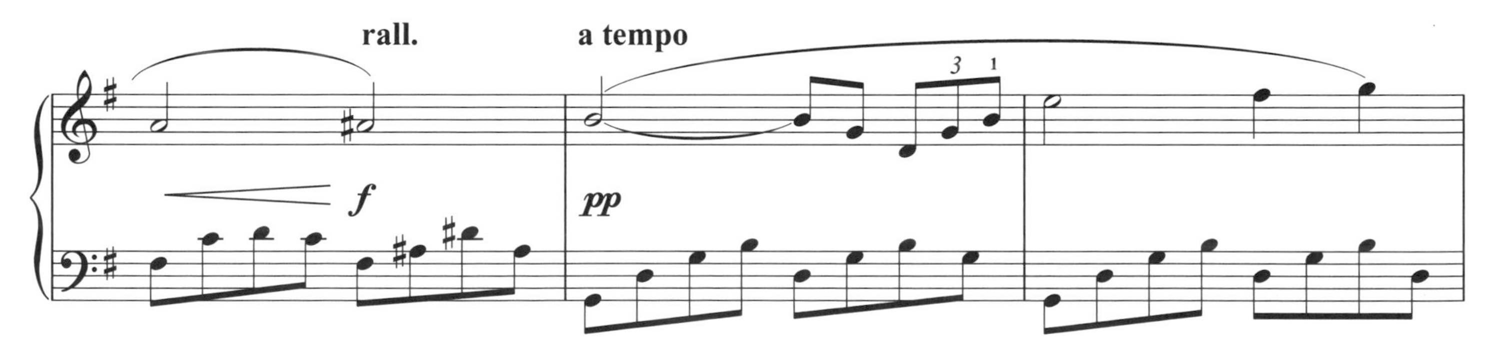


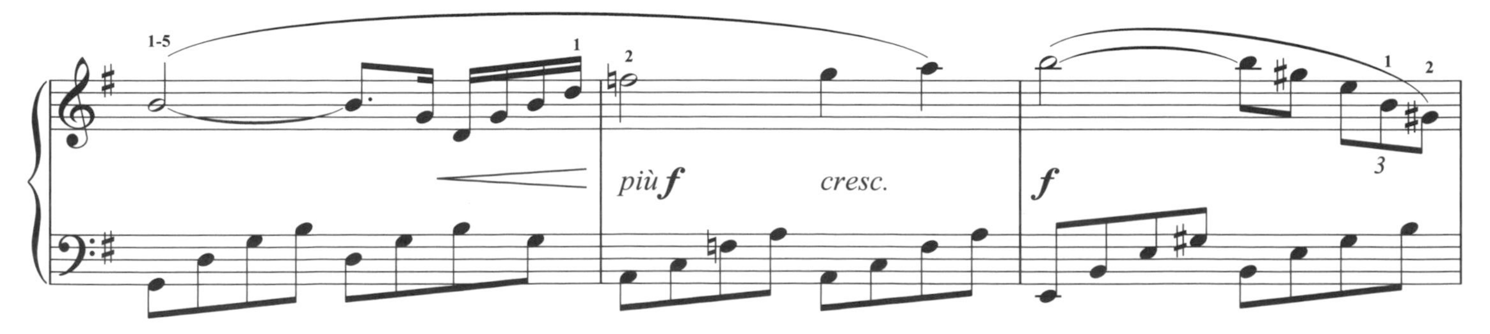

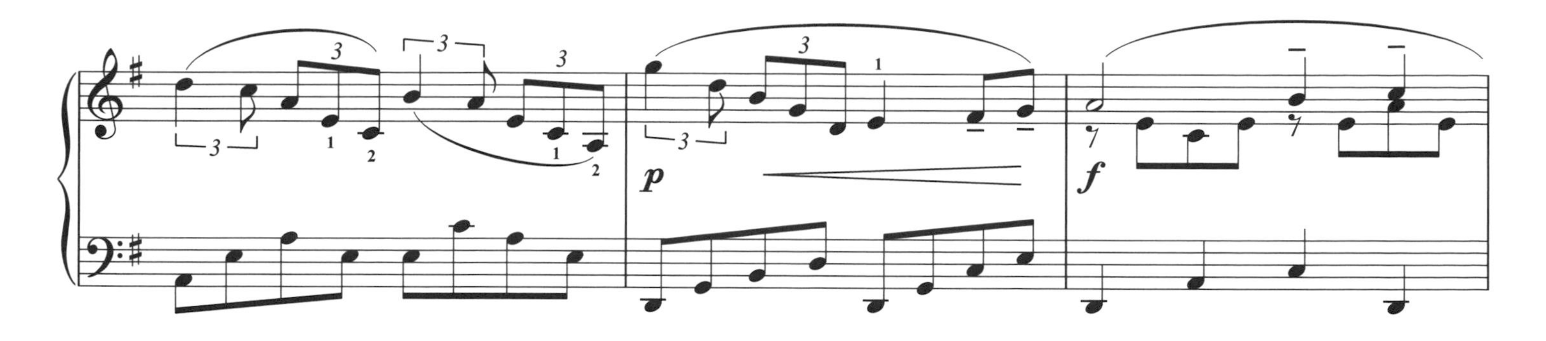
p
f
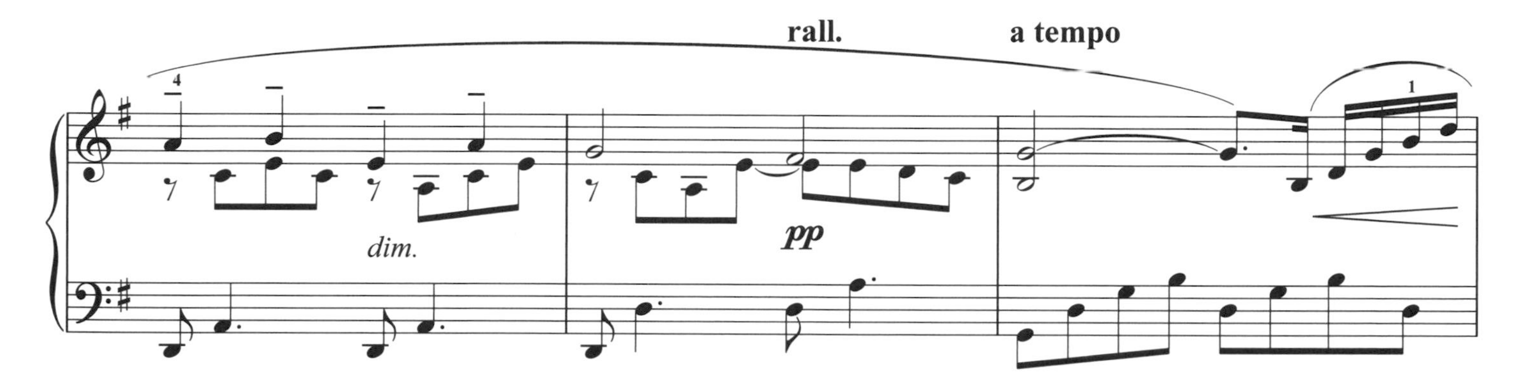
rall.
a tempo
dim.
pp

cresc.
f
p

f
sf
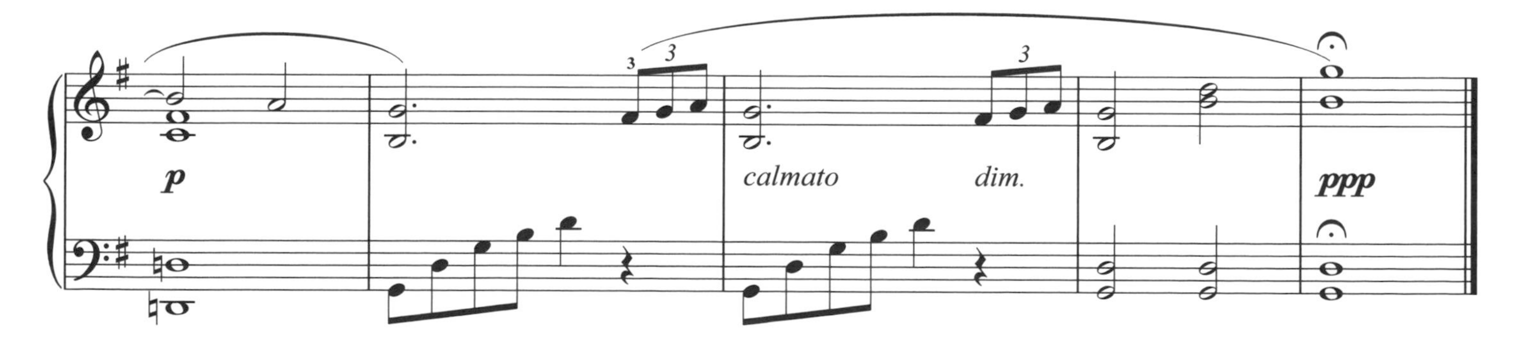
p
calmato
dim.
ppp

# O MIO BABBINO CARO
(FROM 'GIANNI SCHICCHI')

Composed by Giacomo Puccini

Arranged by Jack Long

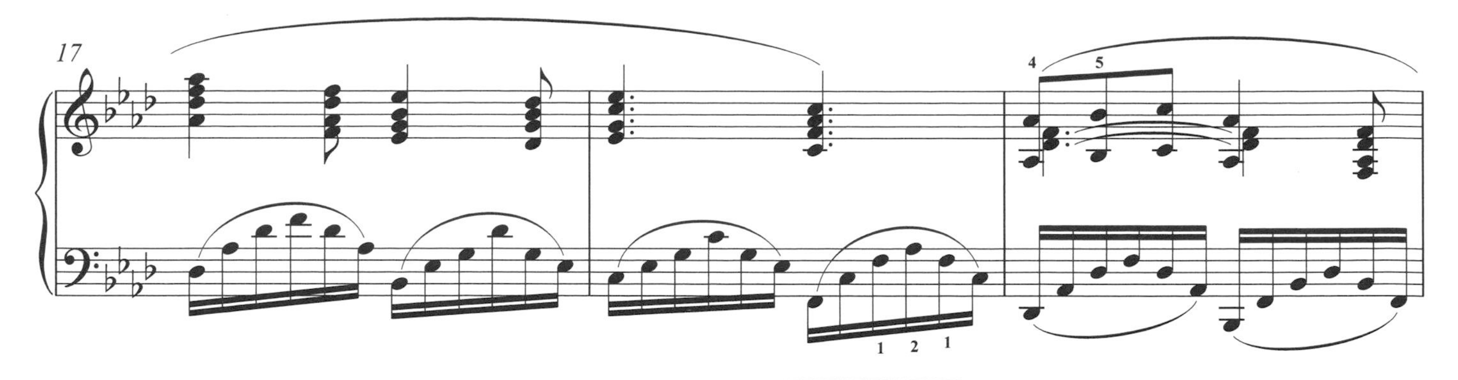
17

20

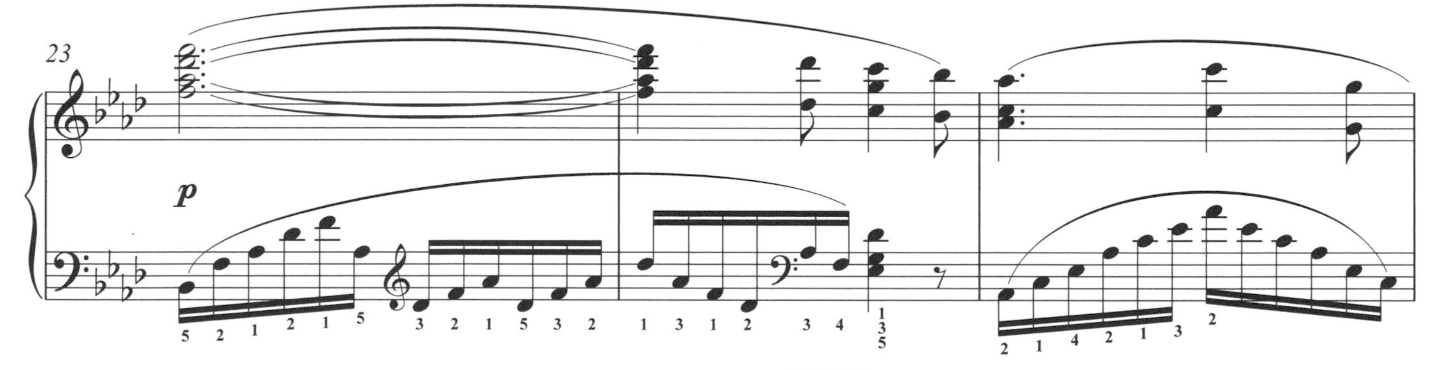
23
p

26
rit.
p
Ped.

29
pp
Ped.

# Polonaise
## (from 'Eugene Onegin')

Composed by Peter Ilyich Tchaikovsky

Arranged by Jerry Lanning

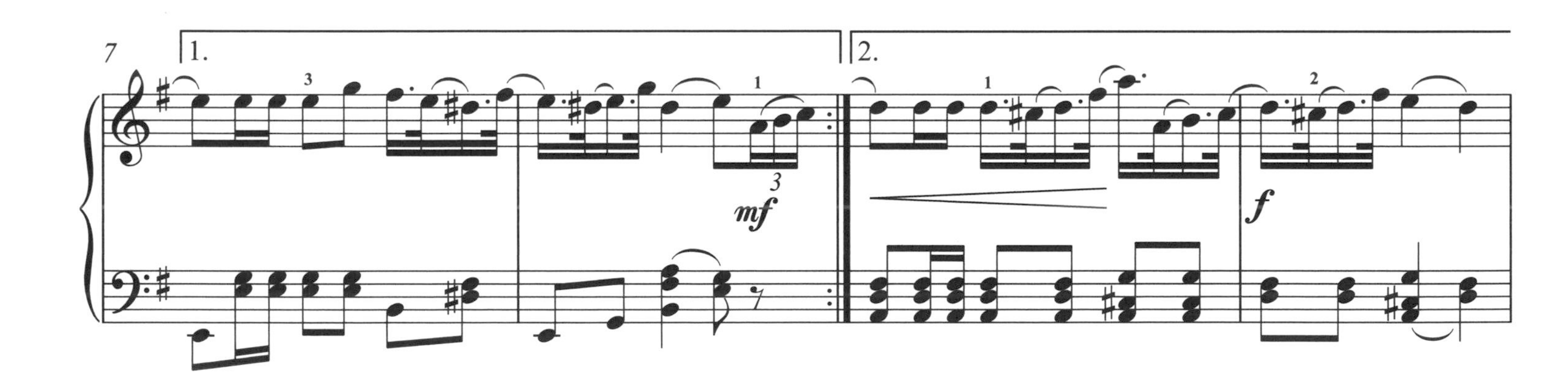


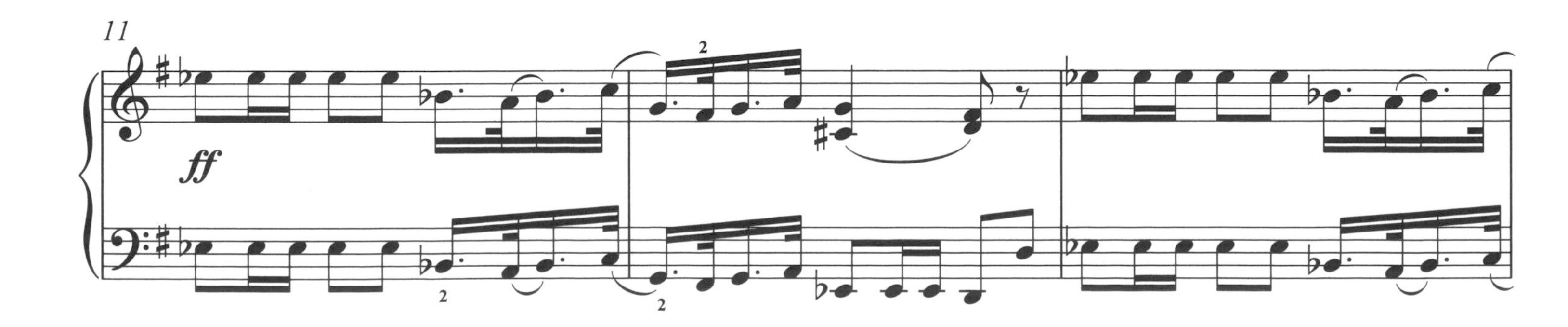

14
(♮)
f
3
cresc.

18
ff
3
1 3
mf

22
1
2
2
2

25
cresc.
f

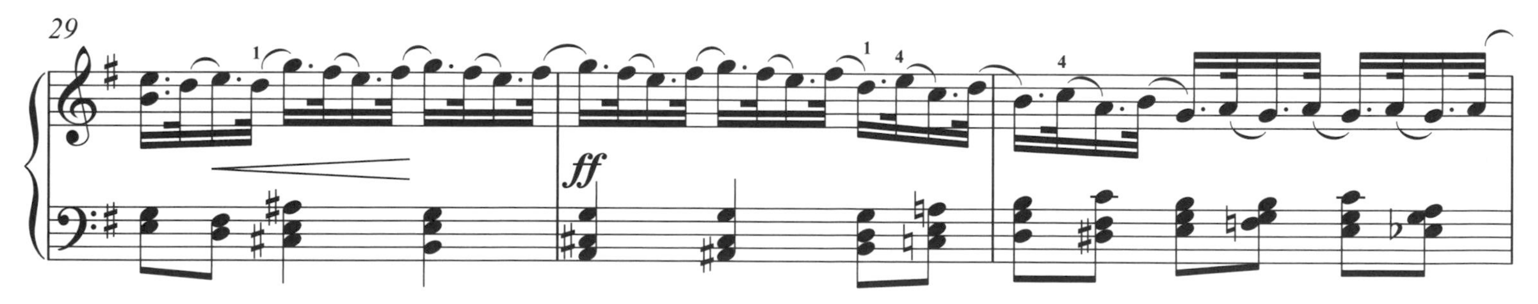
29
1
ff
1 4
4

32
mf
4

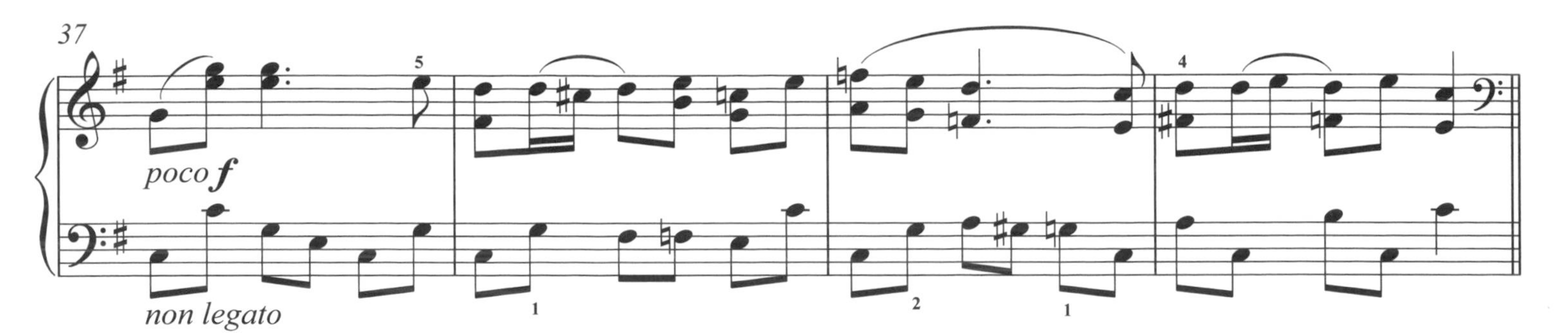
37
poco f
non legato

41
mf (pp)
simile

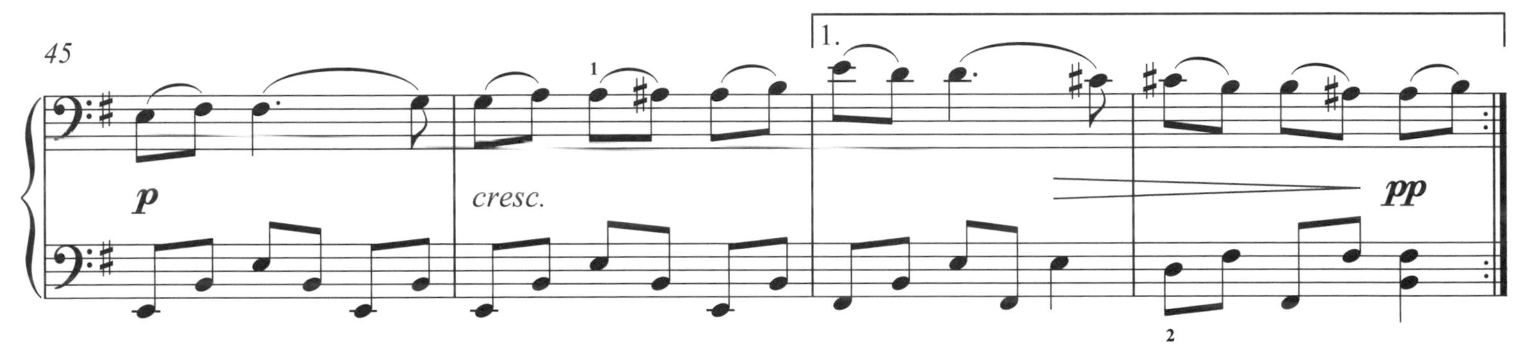
45
1.
p
cresc.
pp

49
2.
mf
f
non legato

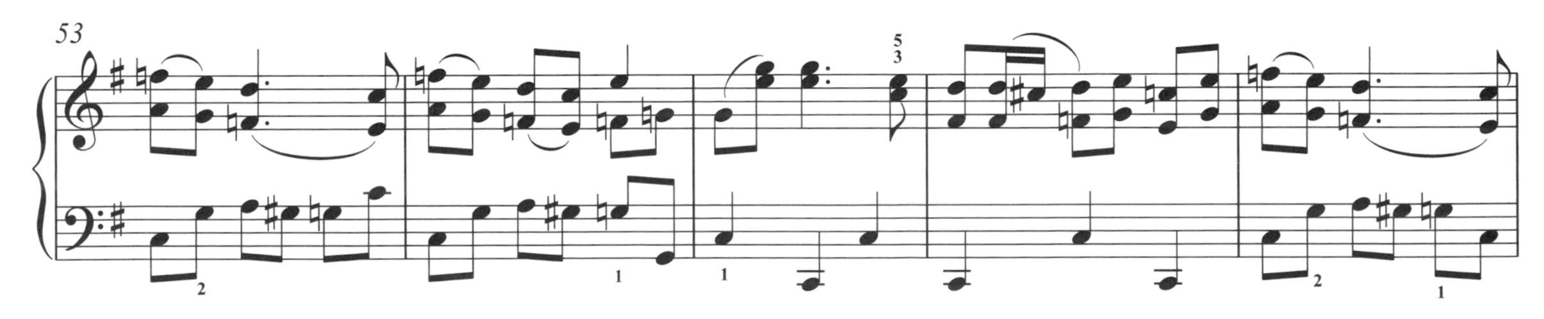
53

58
mf

62

66
f

69

72
cresc.
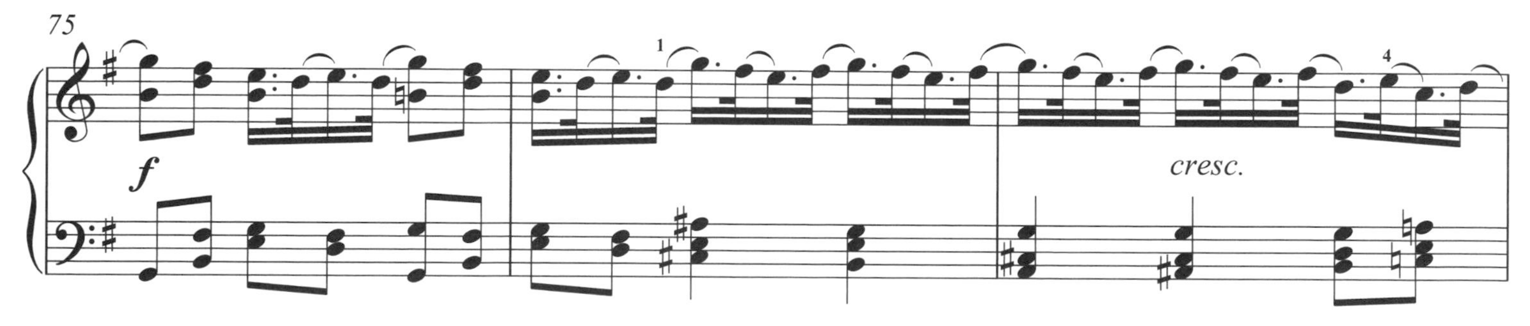
75
f
cresc.

78
ff
fff

# The Ride Of The Valkyries
## (from 'Die Walküre')

Composed by Richard Wagner

Arranged by Jerry Lanning

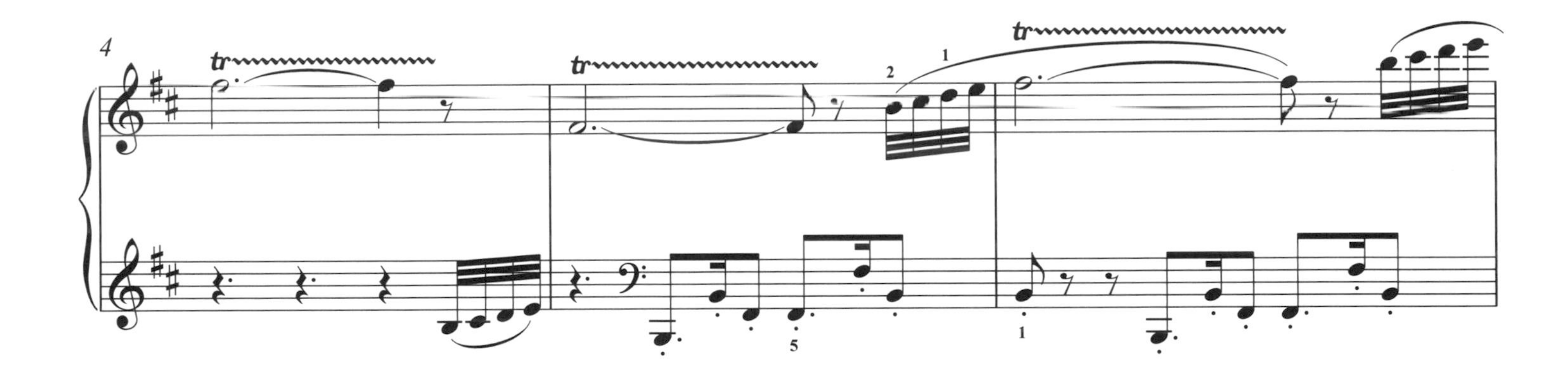

14
1
1

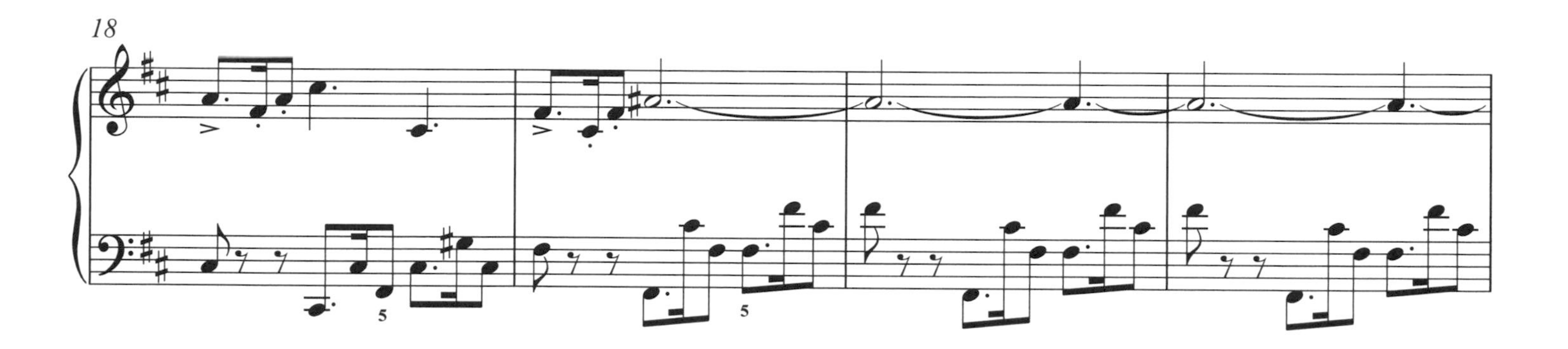
18
5
5

22
2
ff

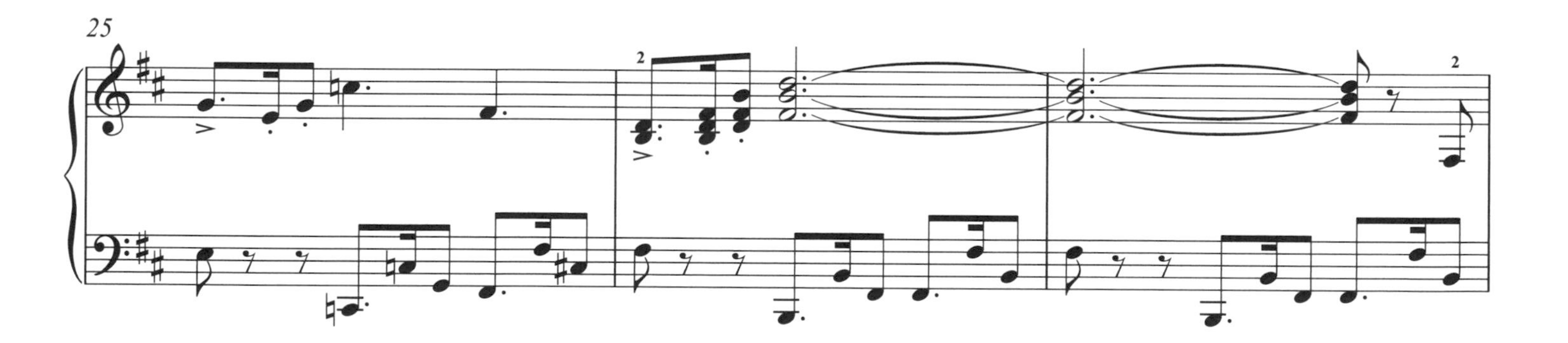
25
2
2

28

31

34

38
fp
cresc.
5

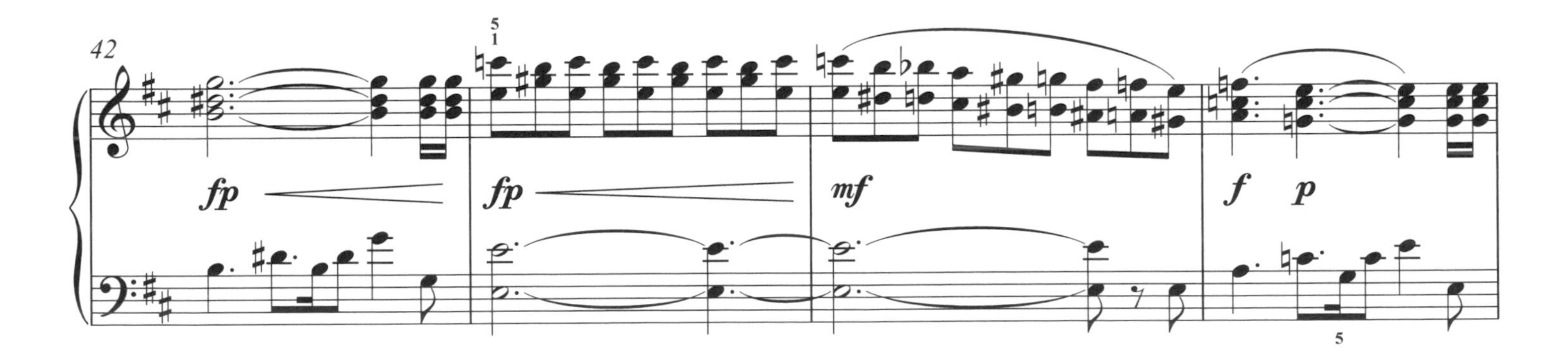
42
5
1
fp
fp
mf
f
p
5

46
5
1
f
p
fp
cresc.
f

49

52
più f
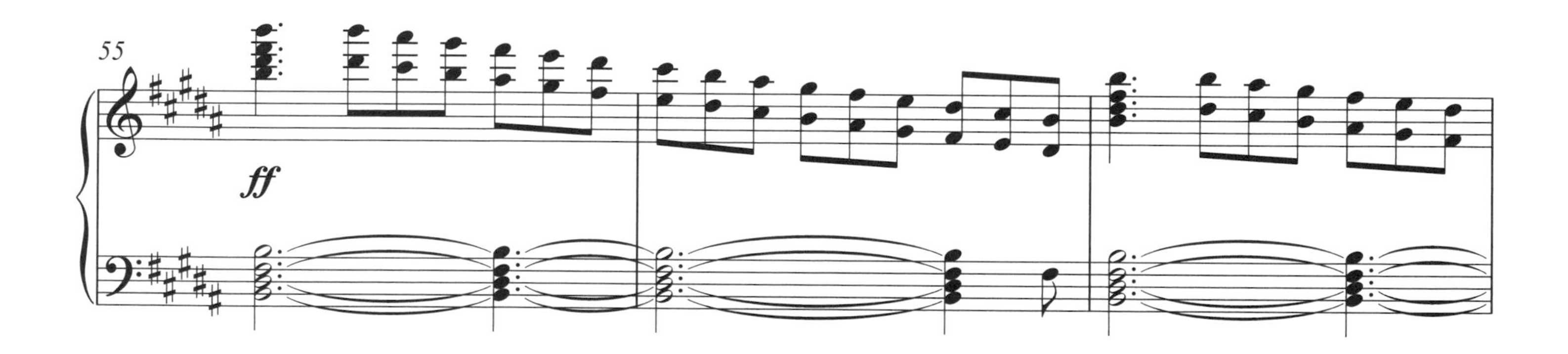
55
ff

58

61

# Sailors' Chorus
## (from 'The Flying Dutchman')

Composed by Richard Wagner
Arranged by Jeremy Birchall



**Animato, ma non troppo allegro** ♩ = 80

21
f
p

26
ff

31
3
3
3
3
3
3

36
3
3
3
3

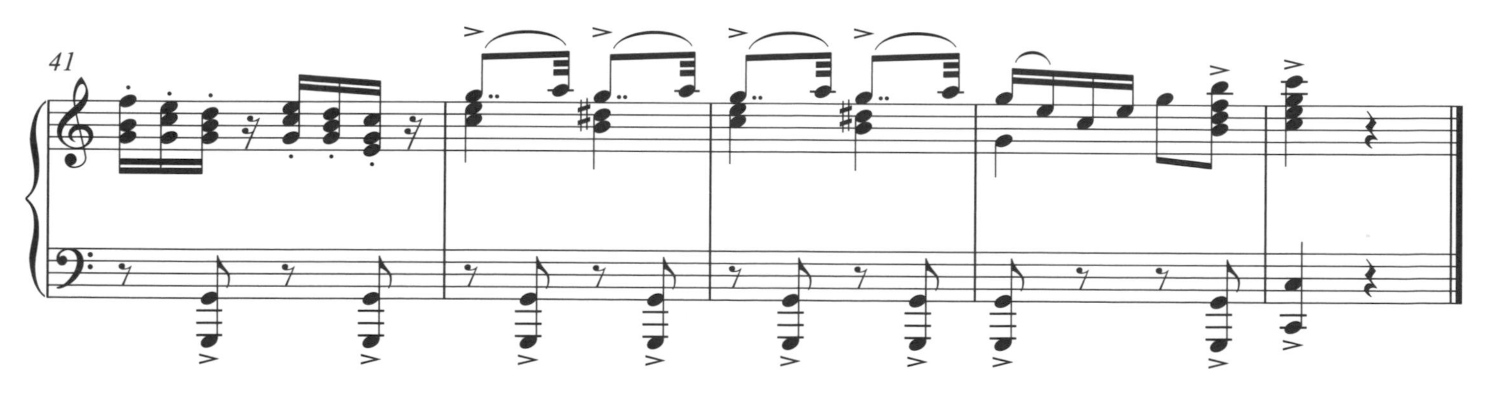
41

# SEMPRE LIBERA
## (FROM 'LA TRAVIATA')

Composed by Giuseppe Verdi



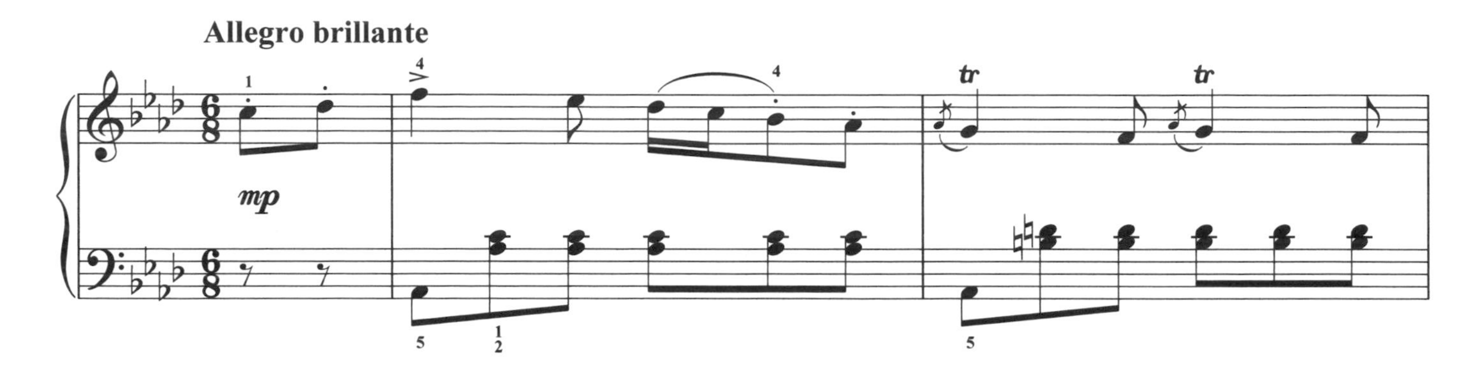


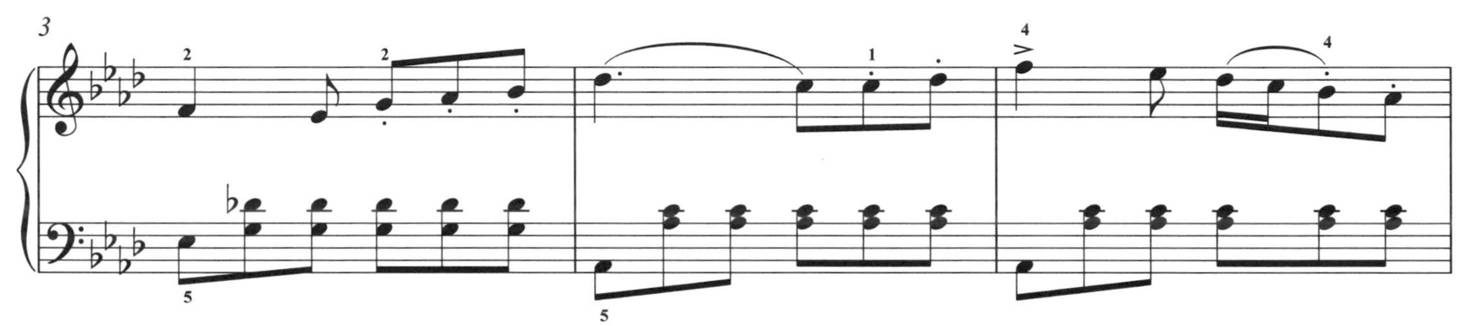

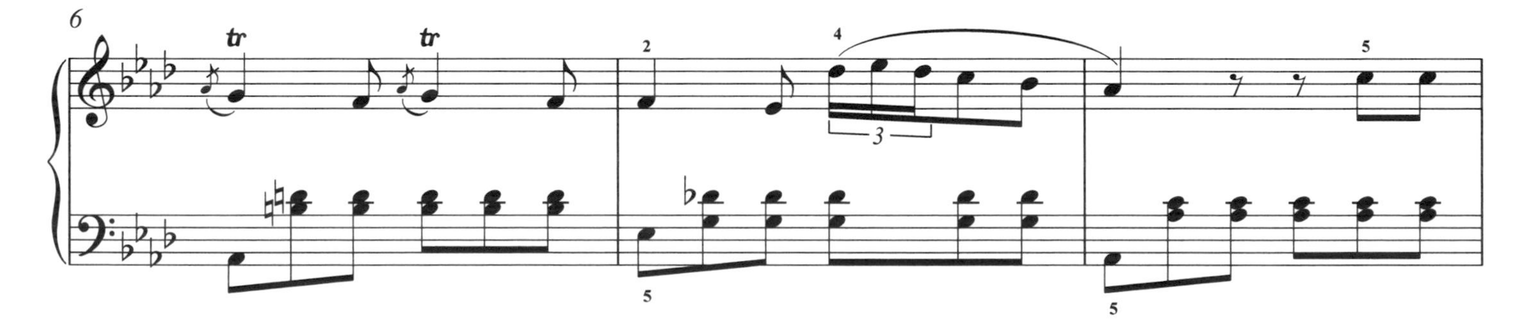


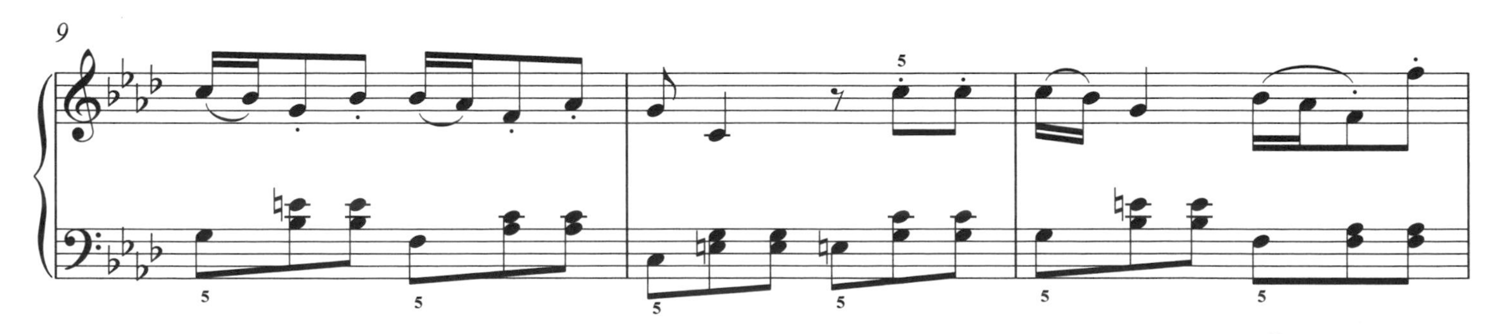

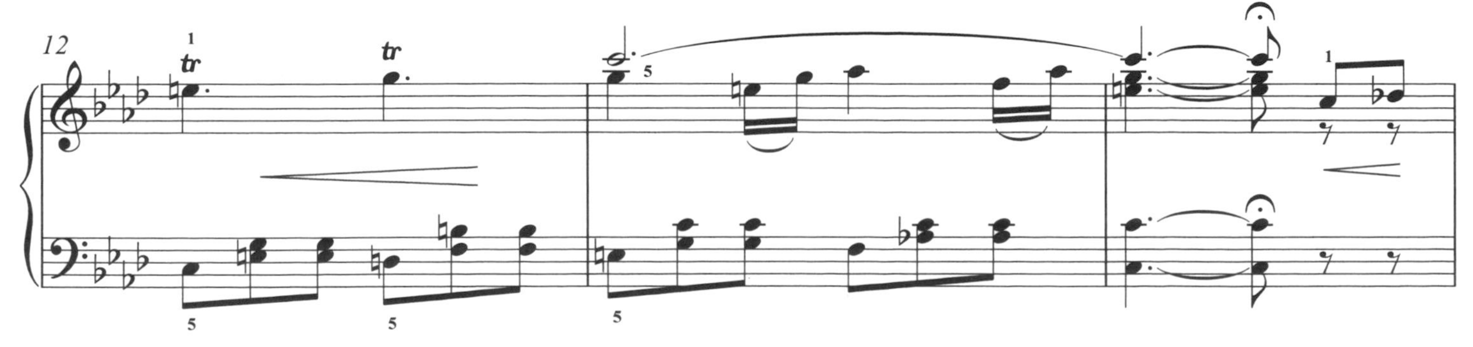

15
tr
tr
f

18

21

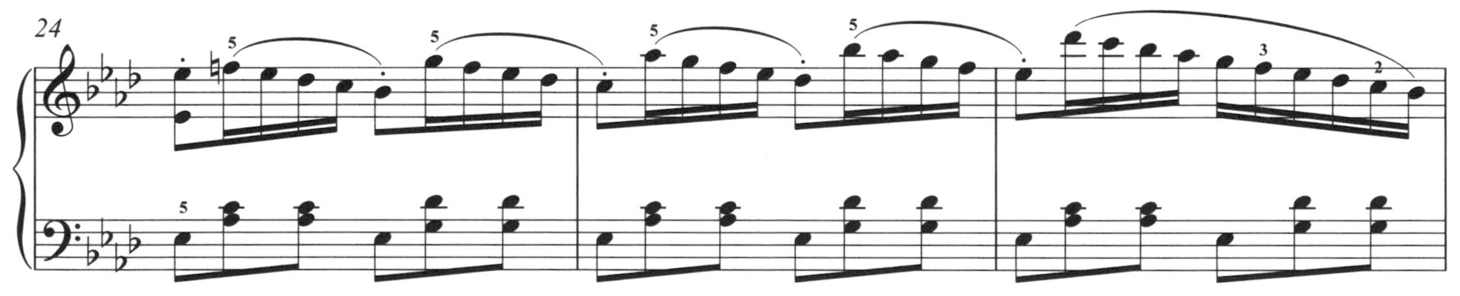
24

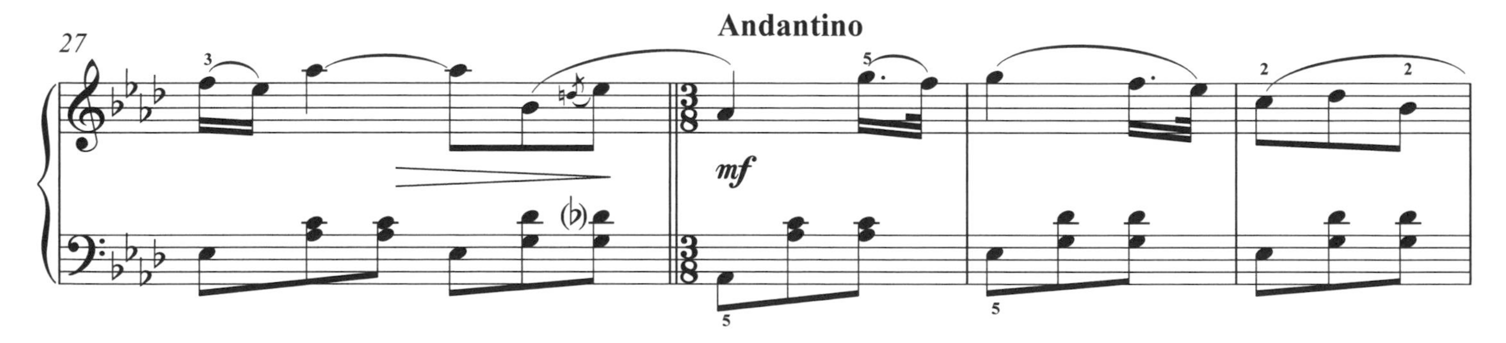
27
Andantino
mf

31
mp

# To The Evening Star
## (from 'Tannhäuser')

Composed by Richard Wagner

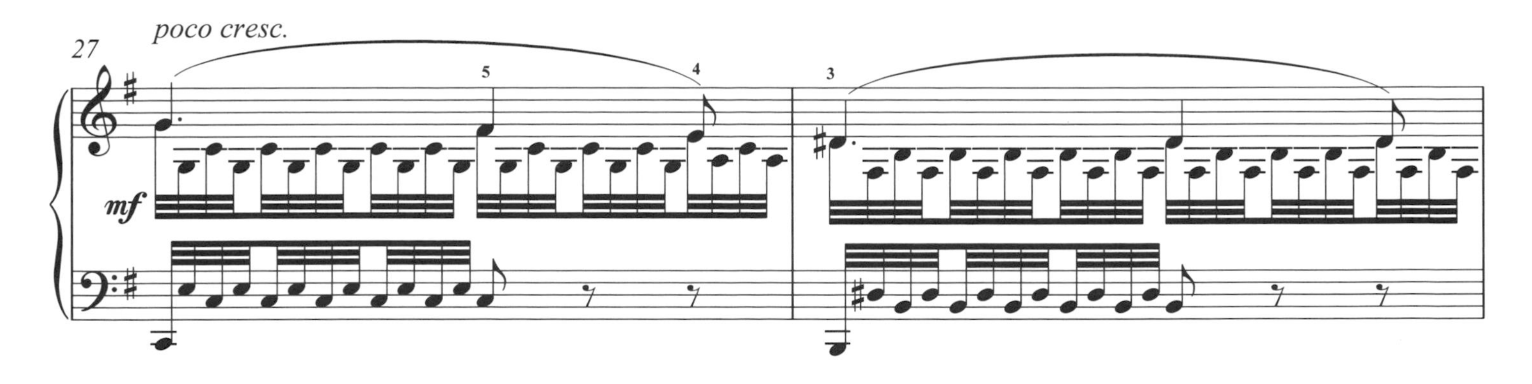
27
poco cresc.
mf

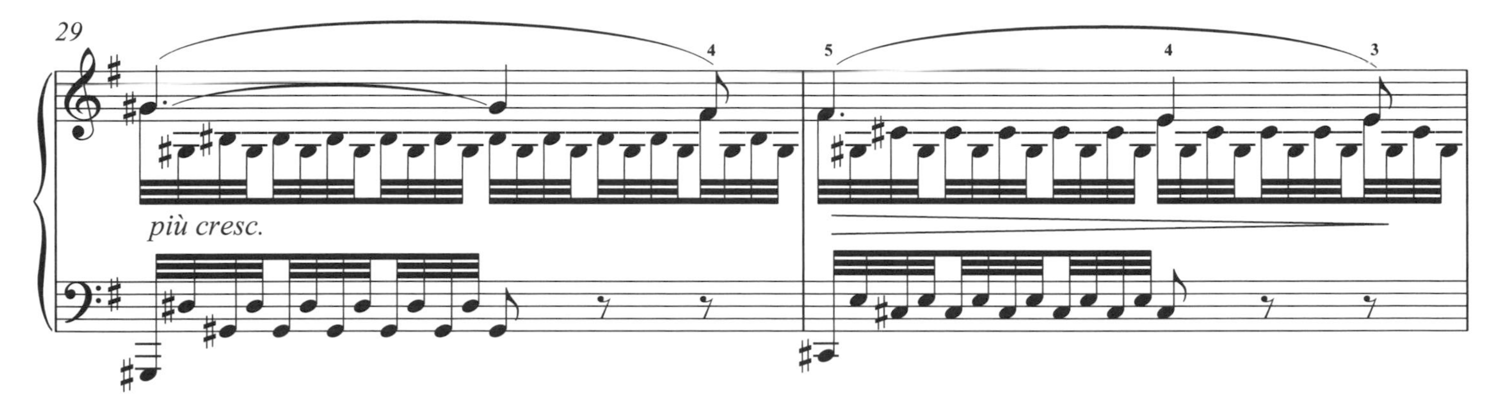
29
più cresc.

31
sempre cresc.

33
f
rit.
dim.

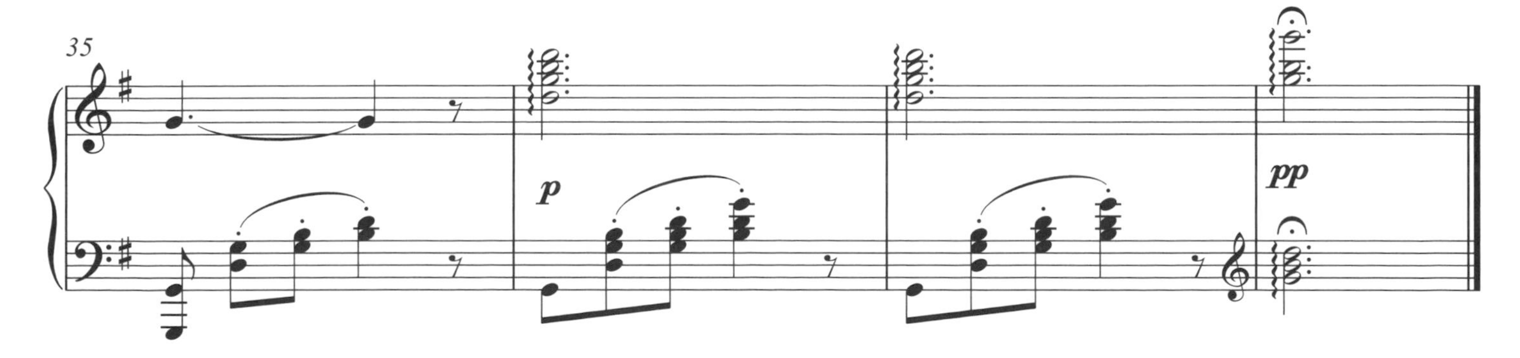
35
p
pp

# Toreador Song
## (from 'Carmen')

Composed by Georges Bizet



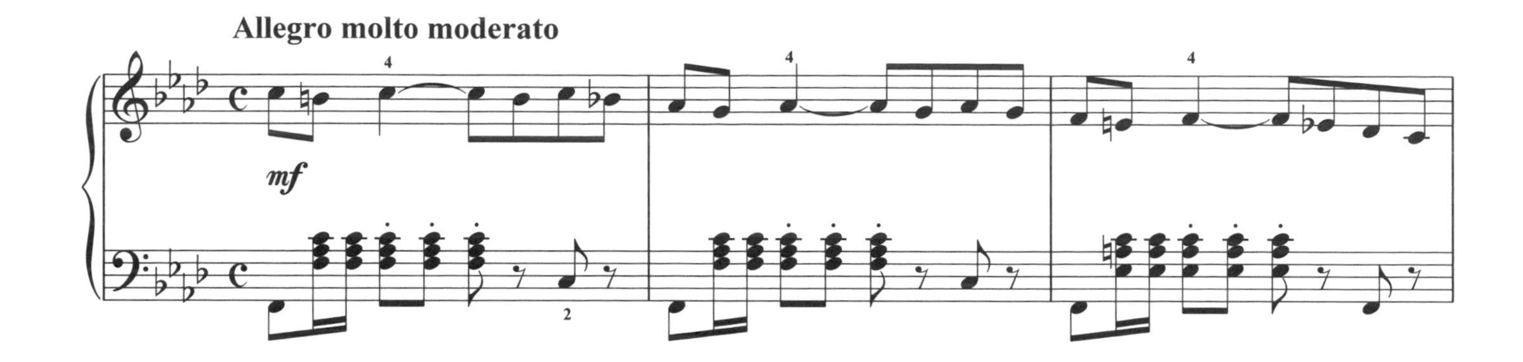

14
p
cresc.
f
ff
mf
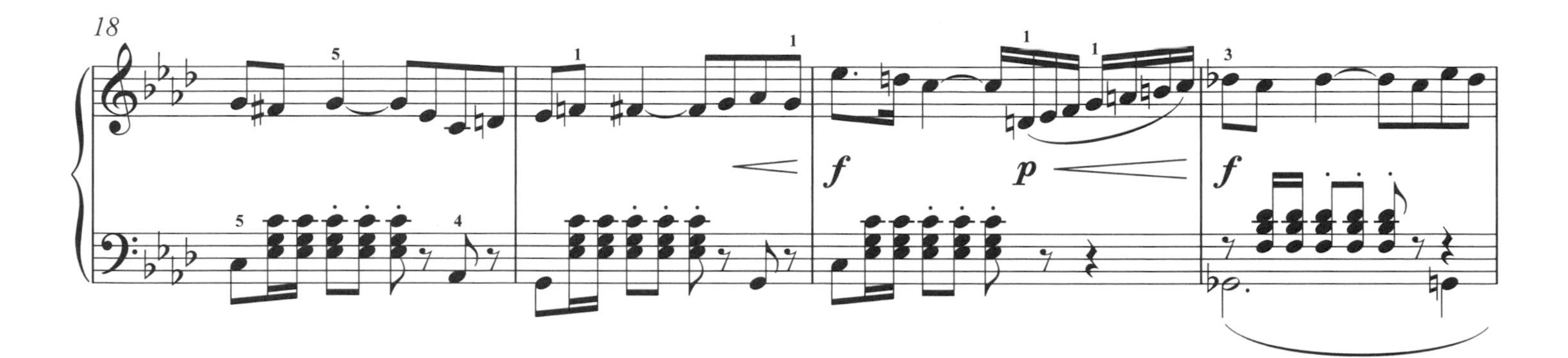
18
f
p
f
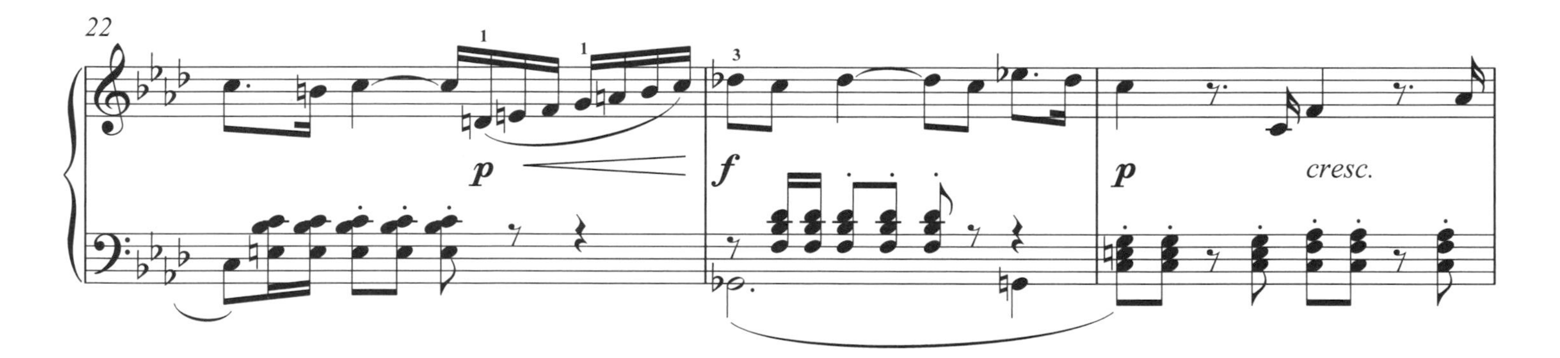
22
p
f
p
cresc.
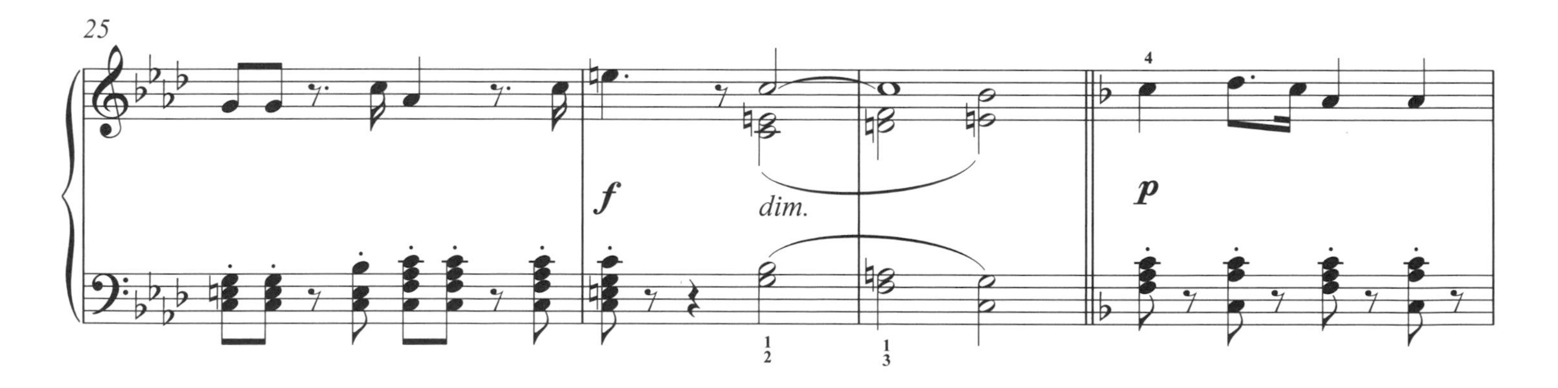
25
f
dim.
p

29

33
dim.

37
p
mf

40
f

44
p

48
f
dim.
pp

# VISSI D'ARTE
## (FROM 'TOSCA')

Composed by Giacomo Puccini

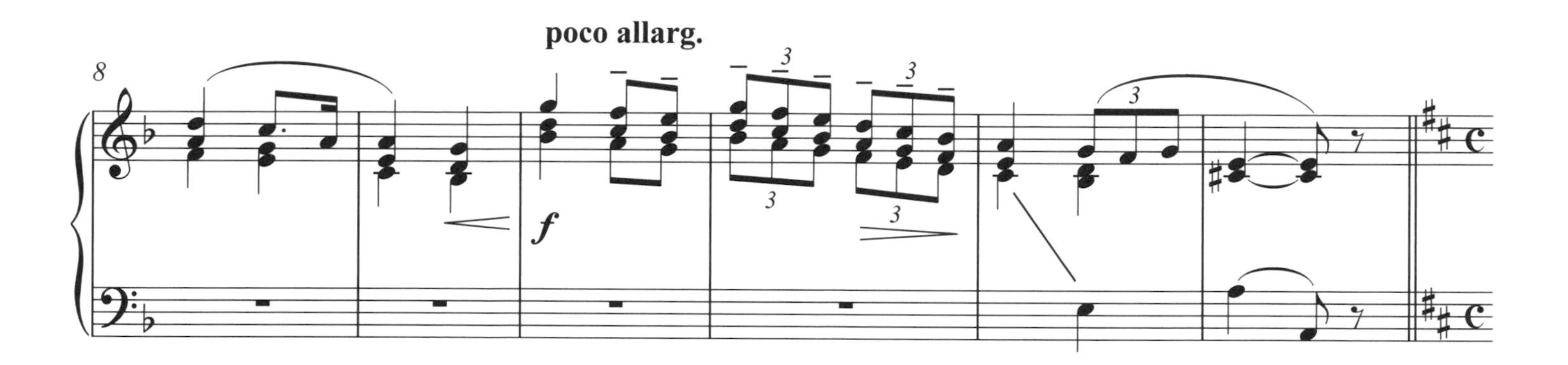

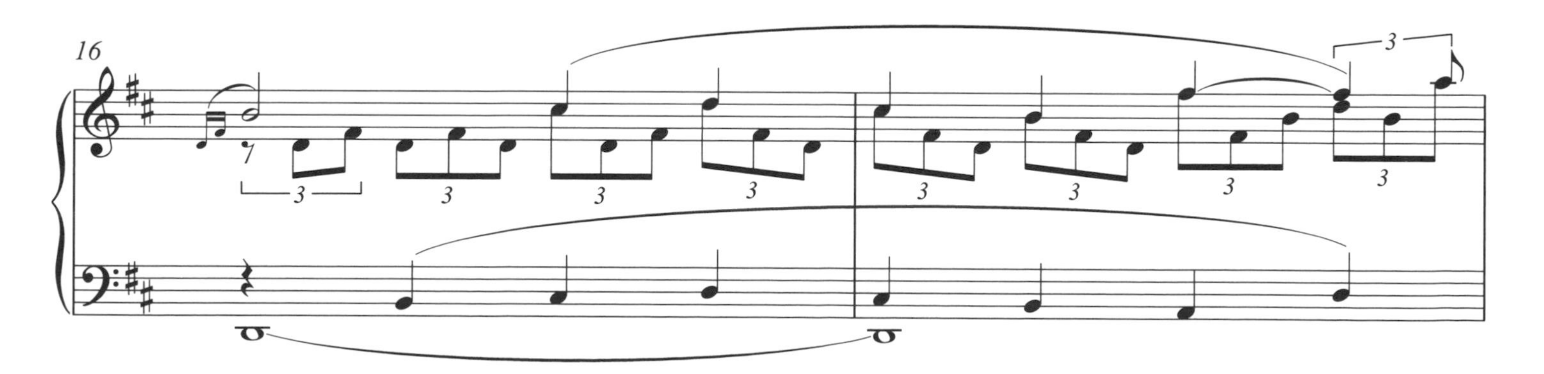

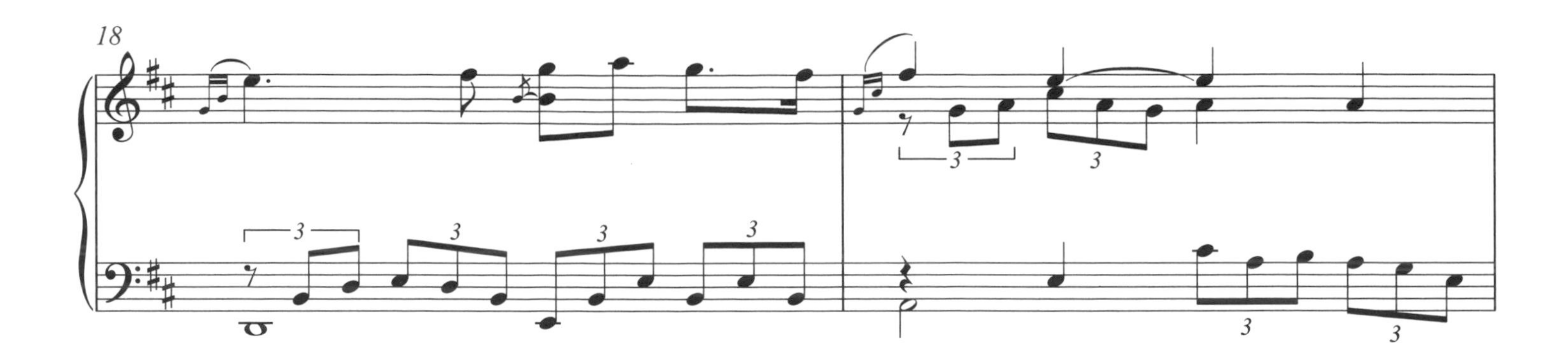
18
3
3
3
3
3
3
3
3

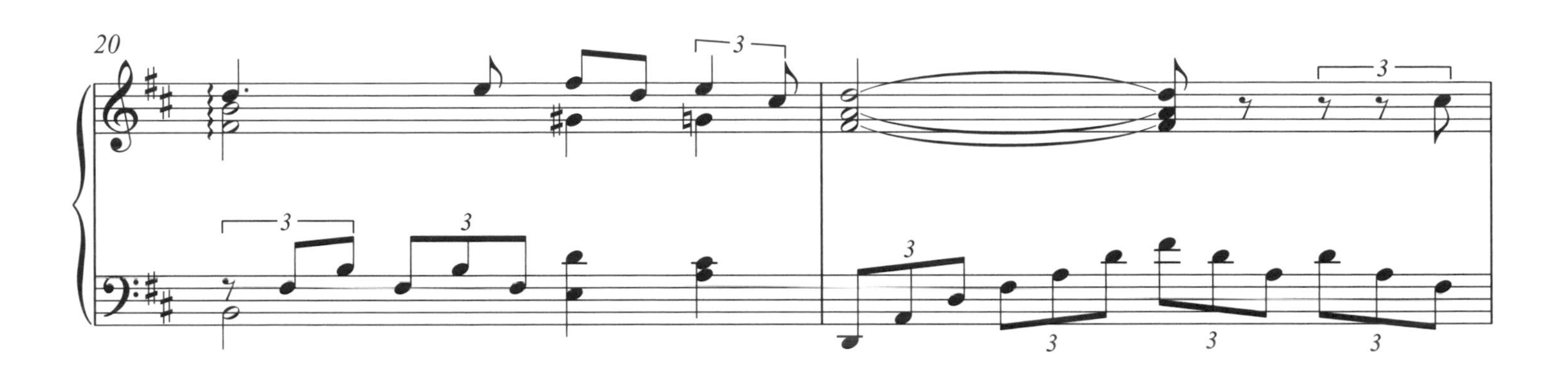
20
3
3
3
3
3
3
3
3

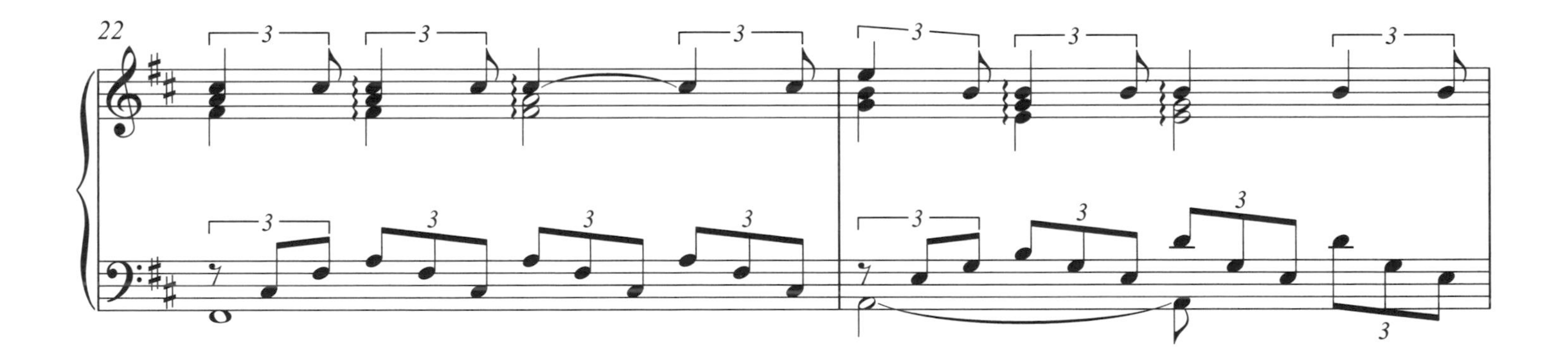
22
3
3
3
3
3
3
3
3
3
3
3
3
3
3
3

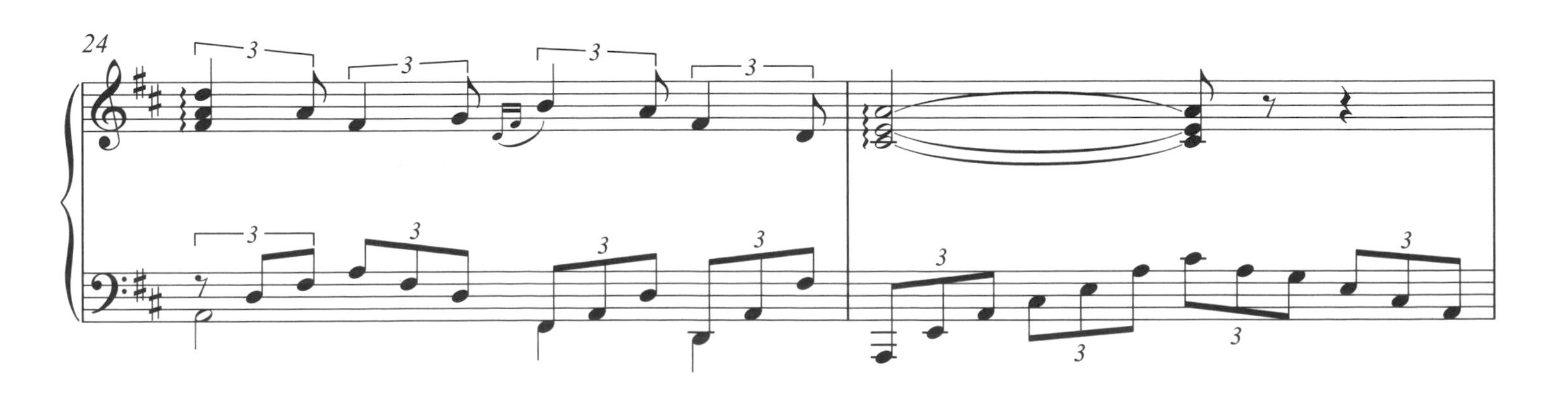
24
3
3
3
3
3
3
3
3
3
3
3
3

26

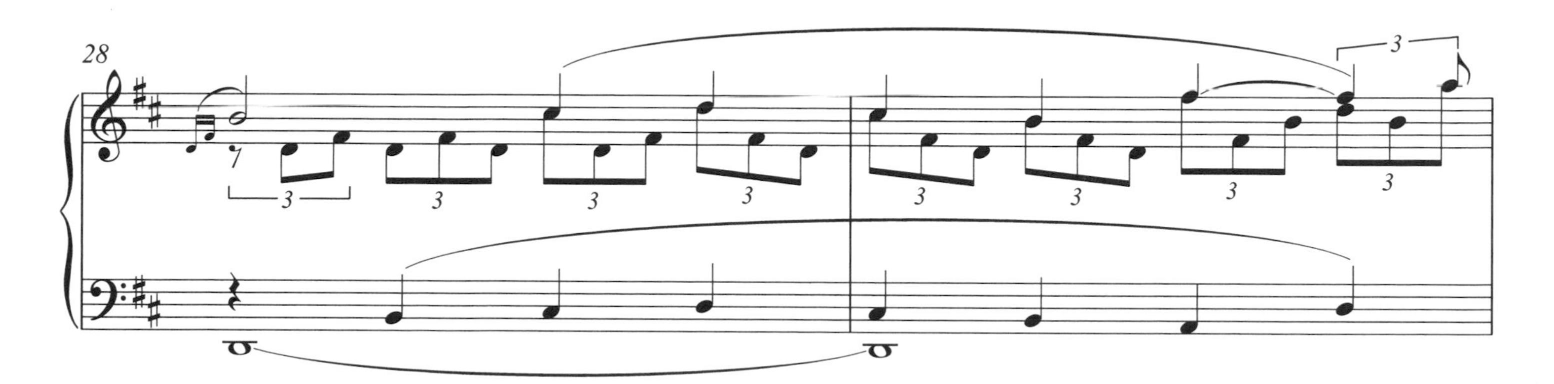
28

30

32
molto allargando
f cresc. molto

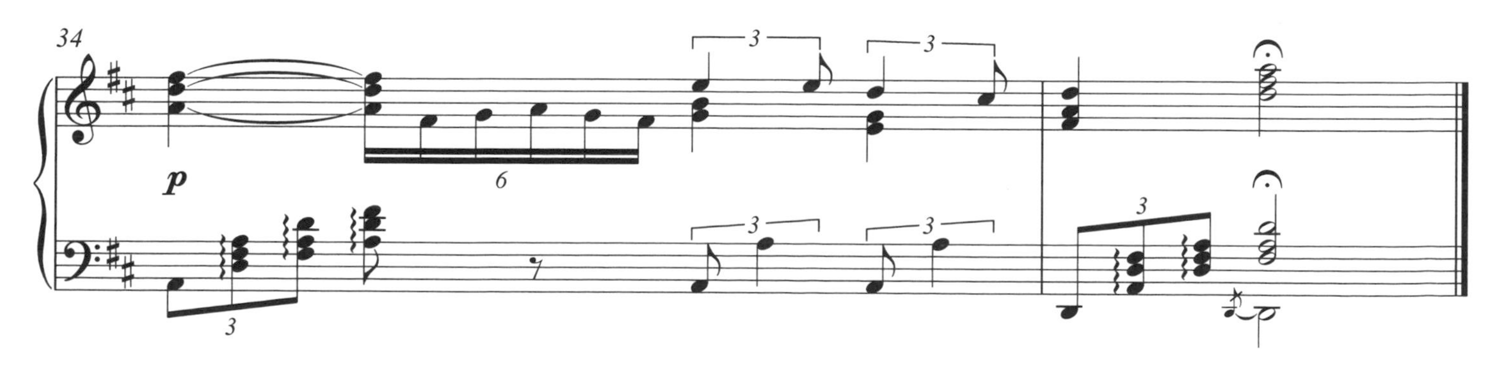
34
p

# Un bel dì vedremo

## (from 'Madame Butterfly')

Composed by Giacomo Puccini



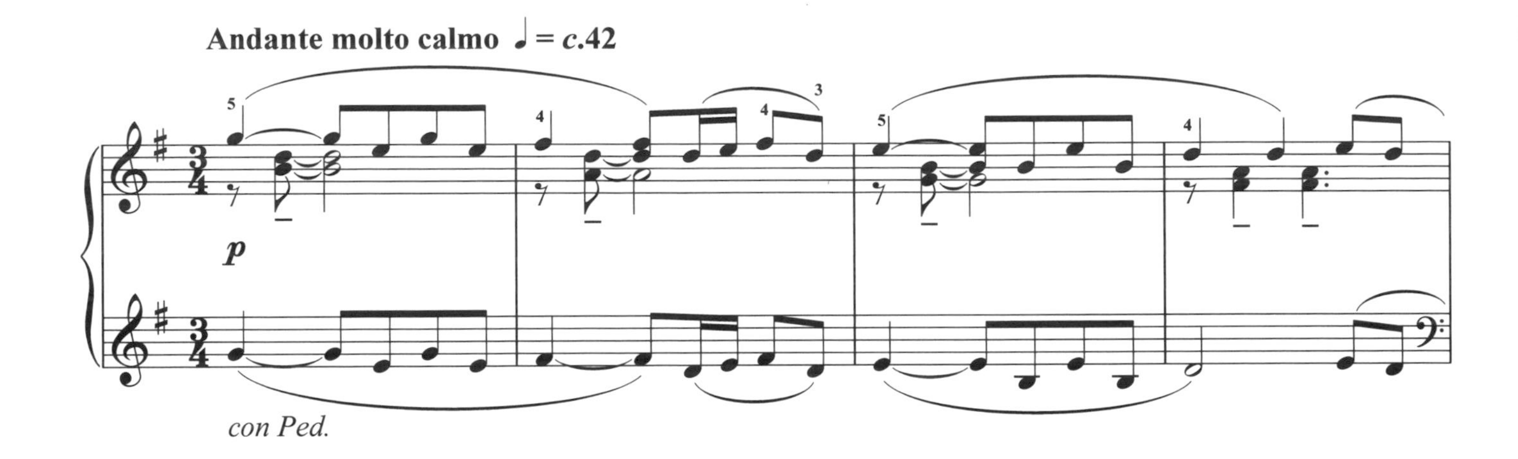

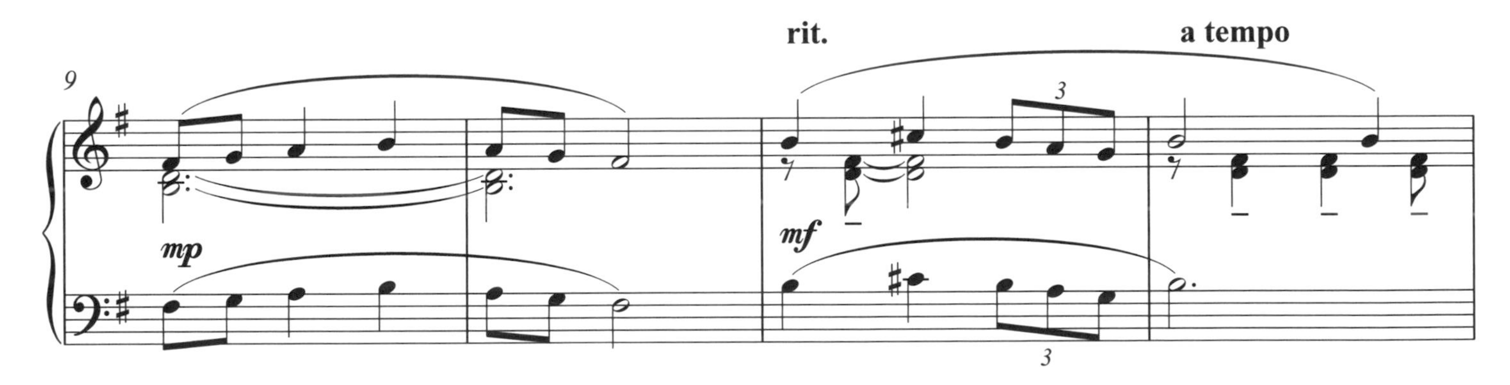


rit.
a tempo
f

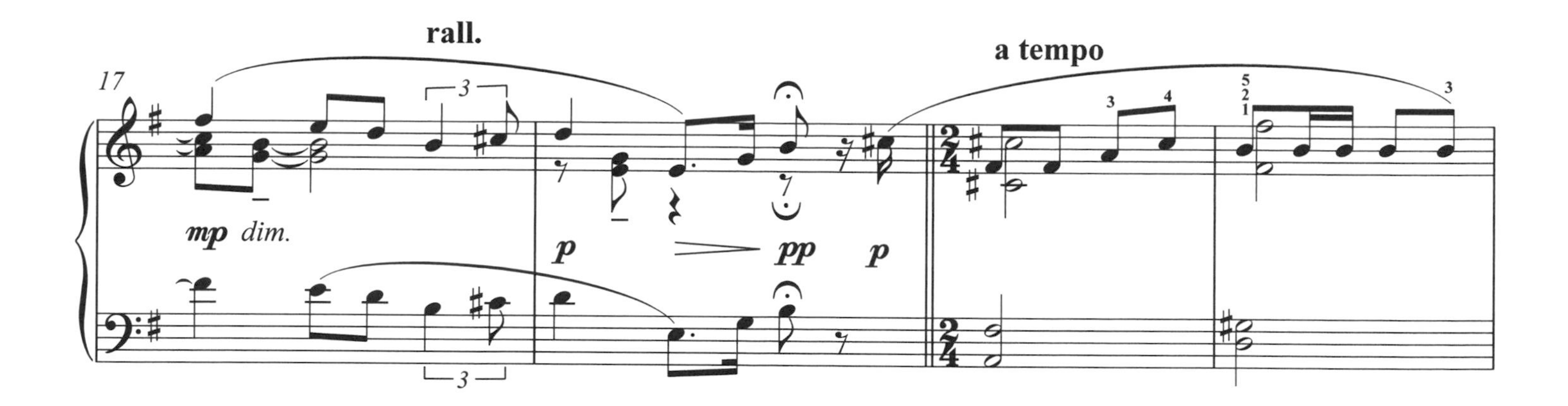
rall.
a tempo
17
mp dim.
p
pp
p

rit.
21

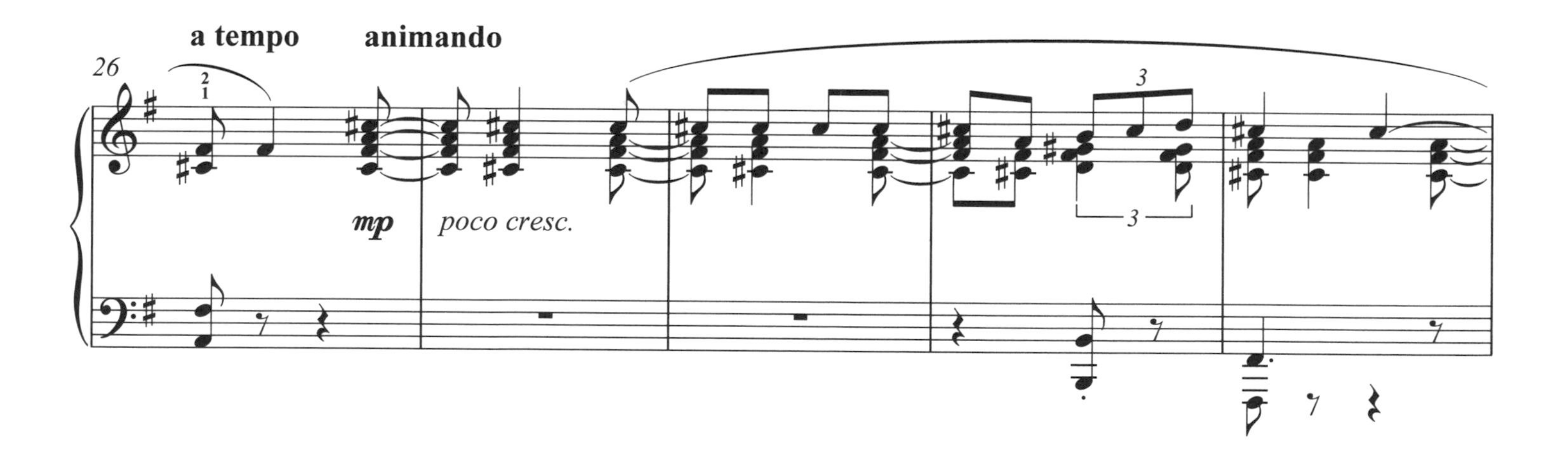
a tempo
animando
26
mp
poco cresc.

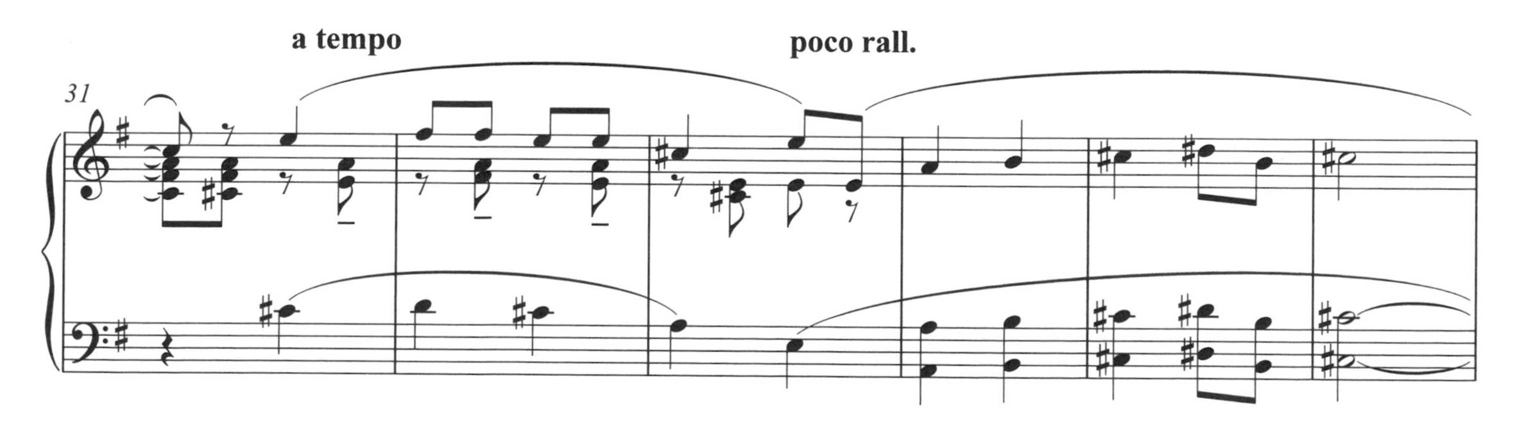
a tempo
poco rall.
31

37
rall.
mp

Lento
molto rall.
42
pp
5-1


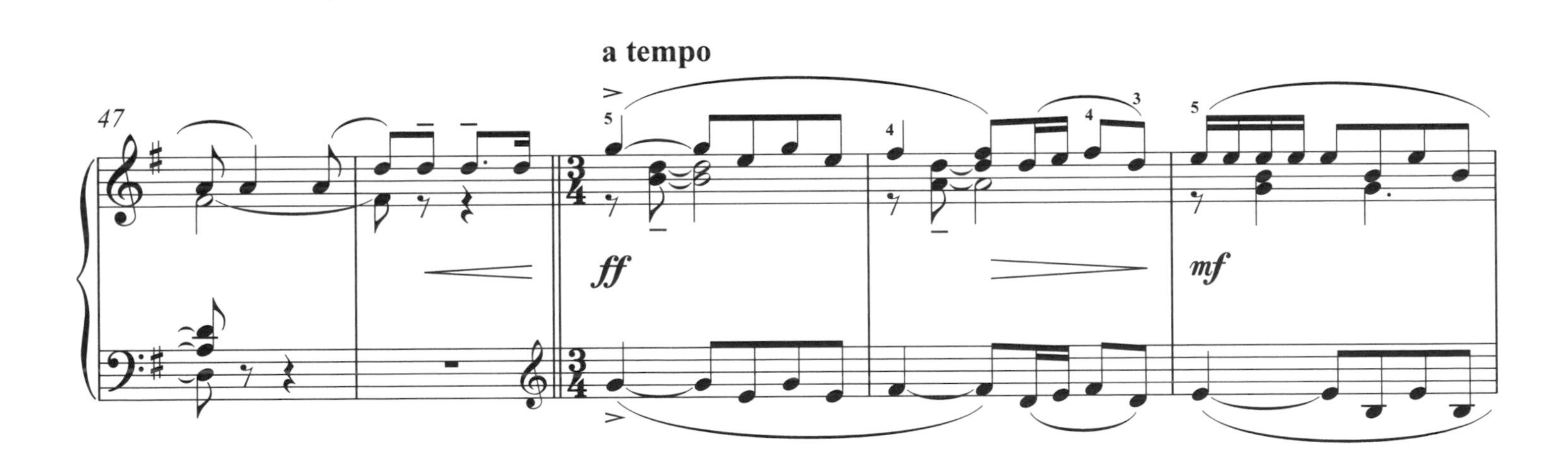

a tempo
47
ff
mf

52
mp

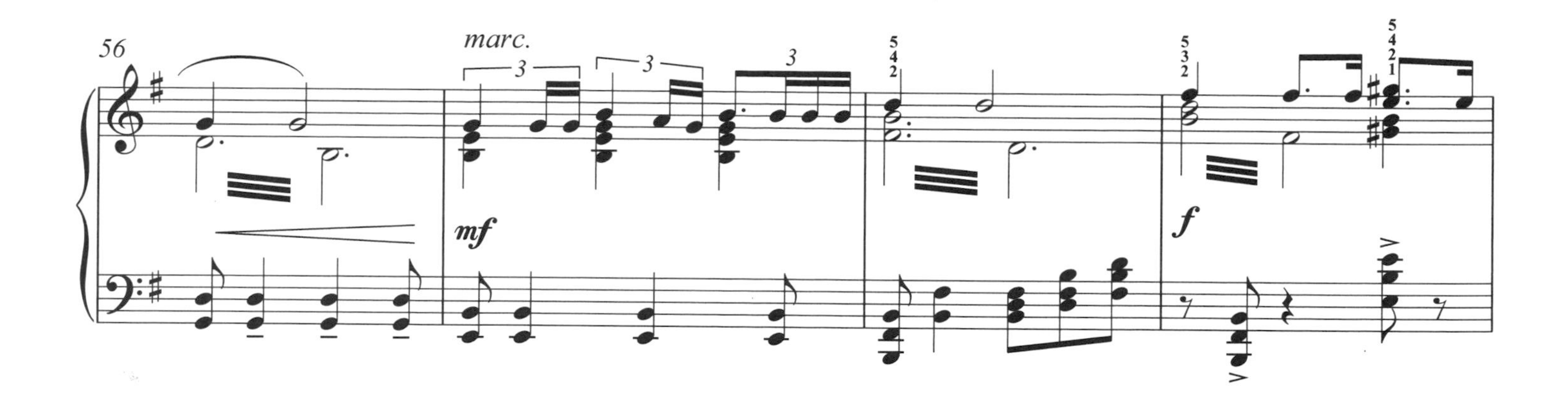
56
marc.
mf
f

60
fff

63
poco a poco dim.

67
p
mf
pp

# Una furtiva lagrima
## (from 'L'elisir d'amore')

Composed by Gaetano Donizetti

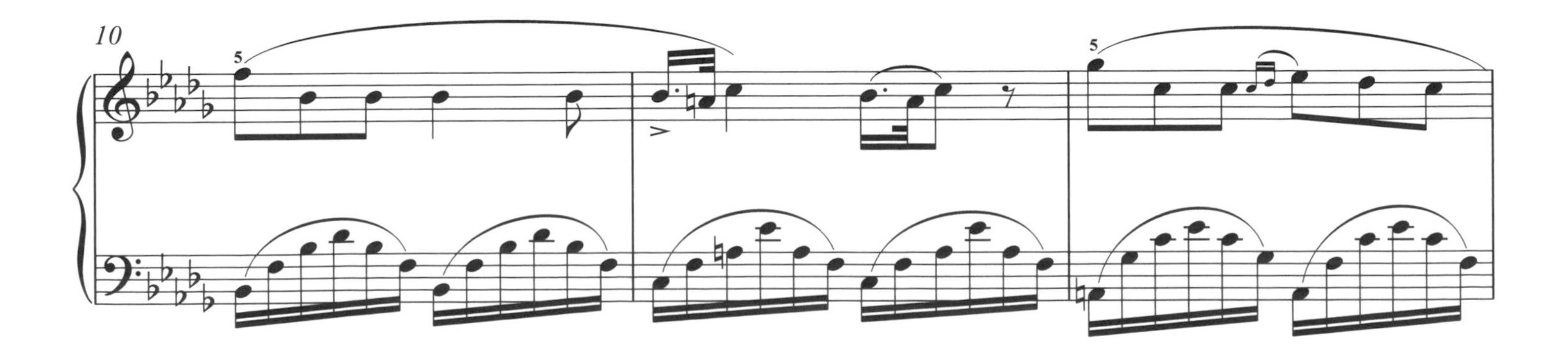

13
4
5

16
2
5

19
4

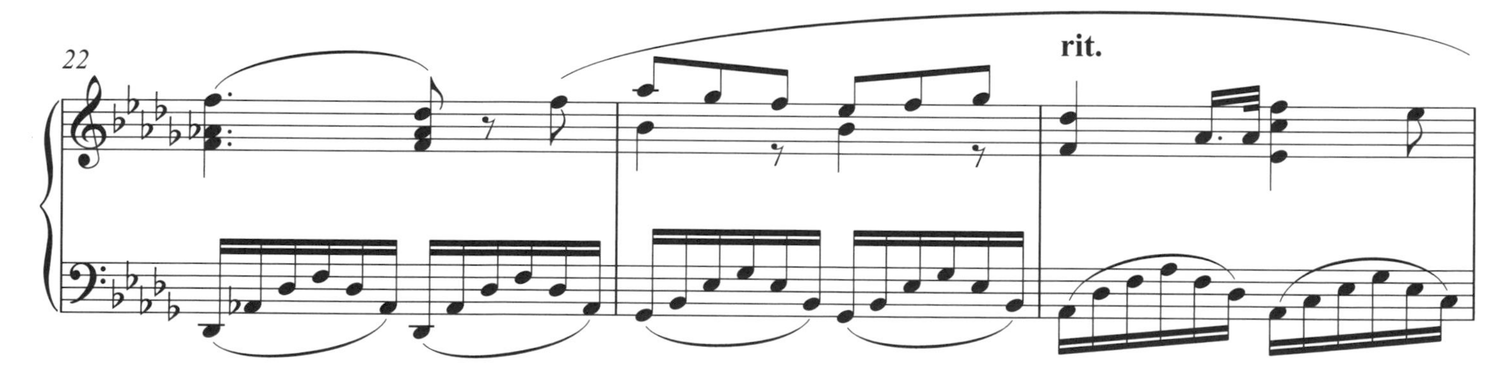
22
rit.

a tempo
25
5
p

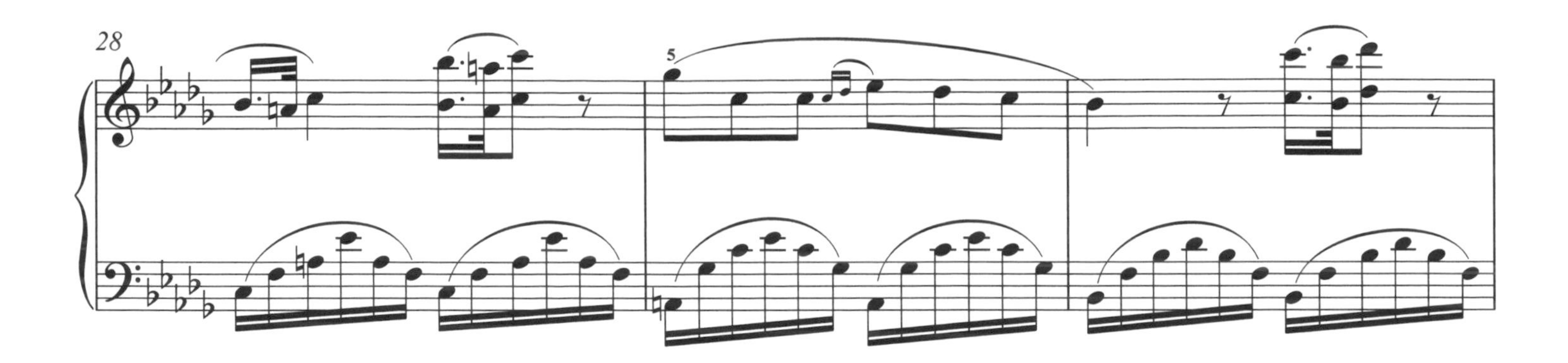
28

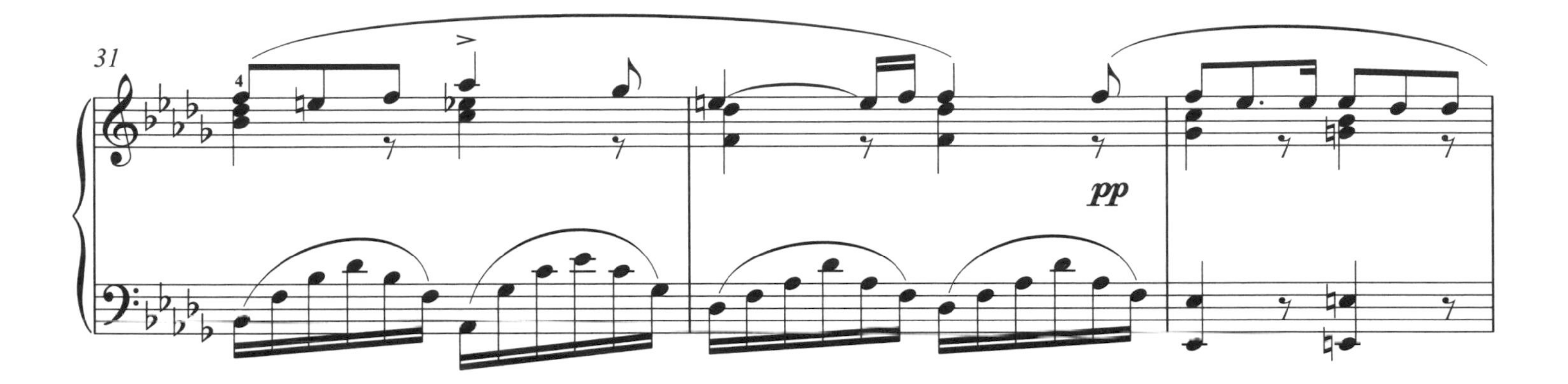
31
pp

34

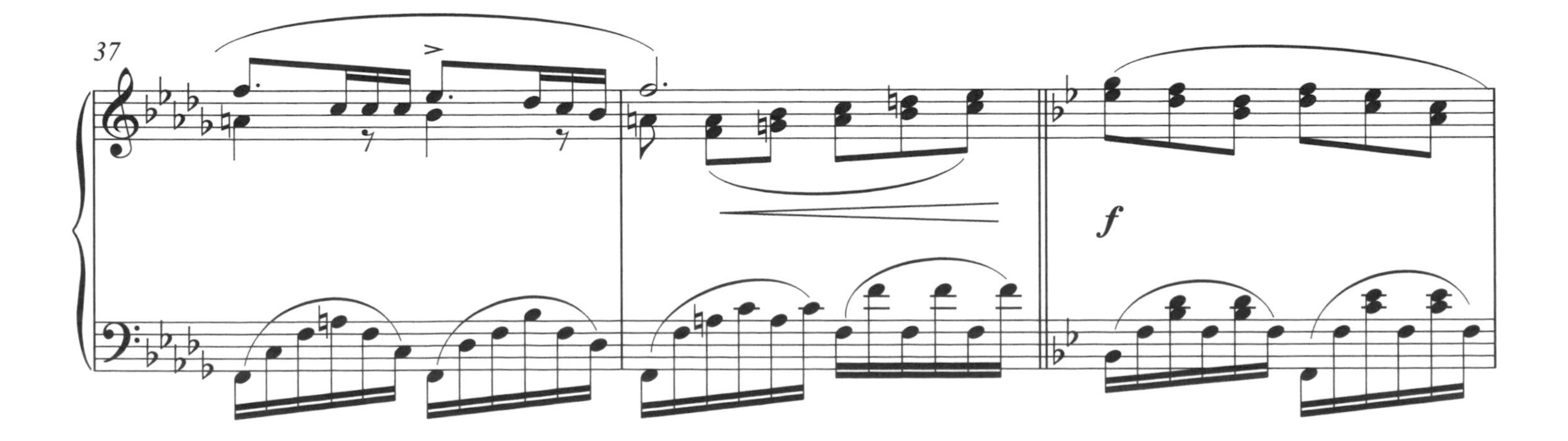
37
f

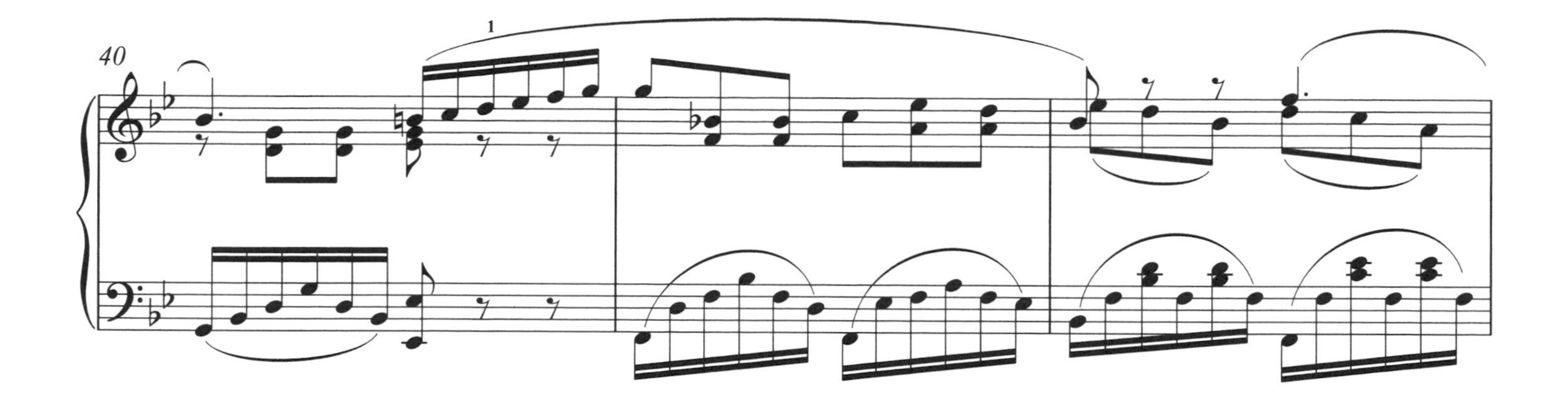
40
1

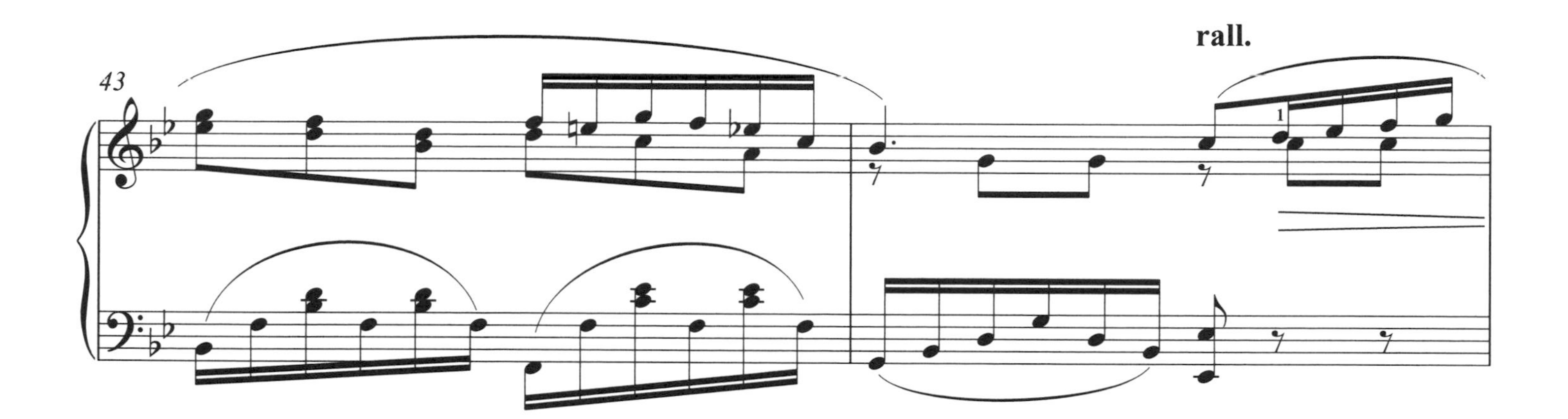
rall.
43
1

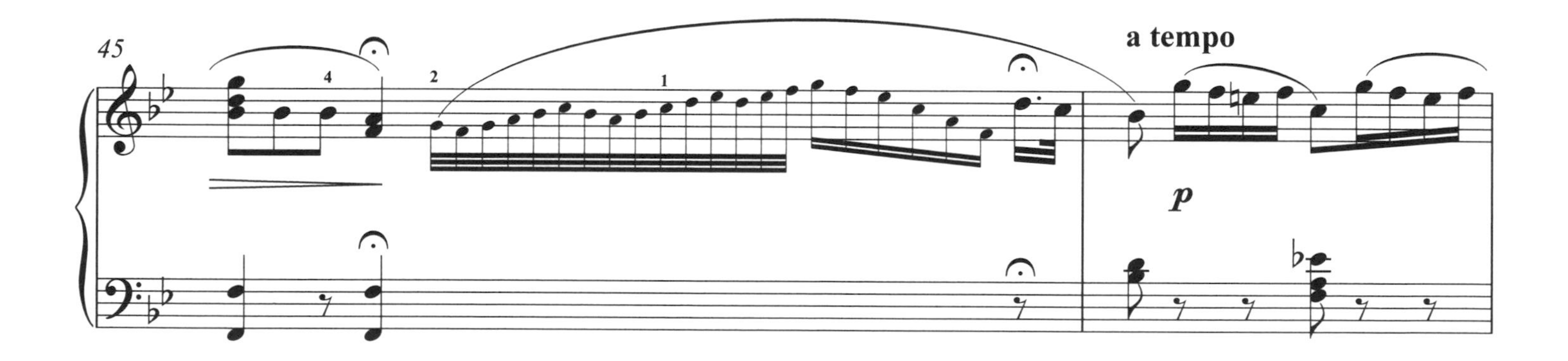
45
a tempo
4
2
1
p

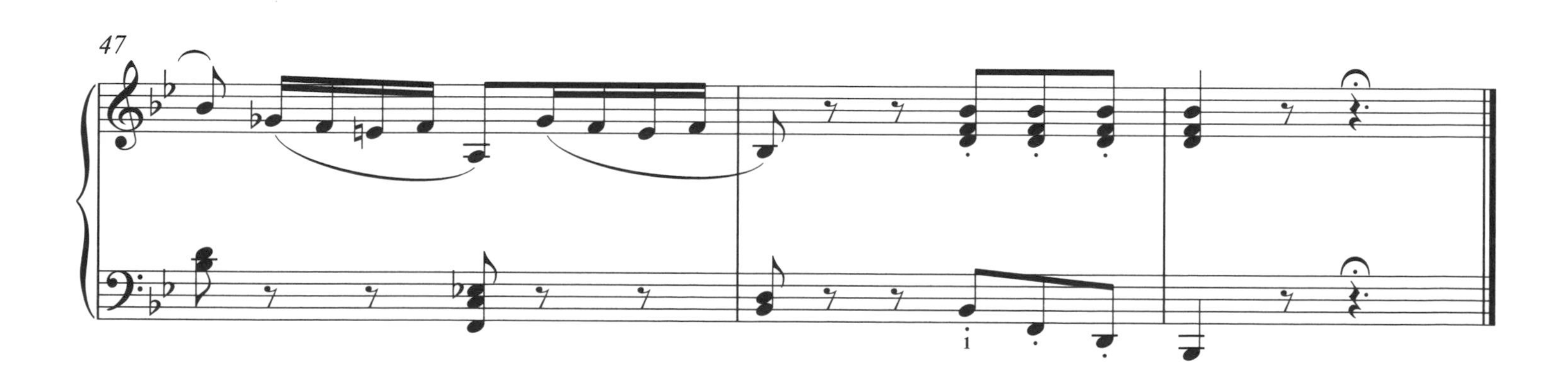
47
1

# Vesti la giubba
## (from 'Pagliacci')

Composed by Ruggero Leoncavallo

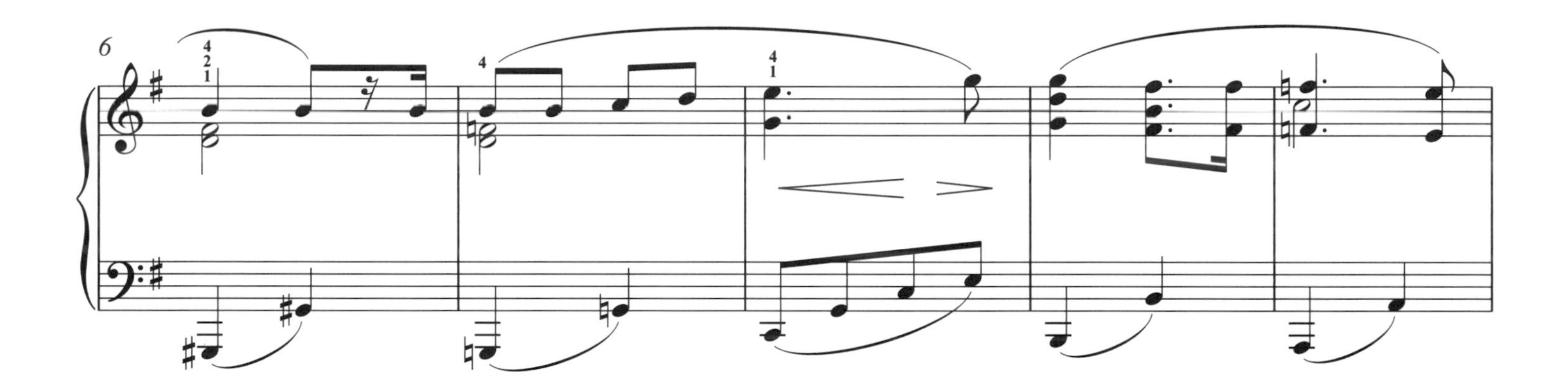

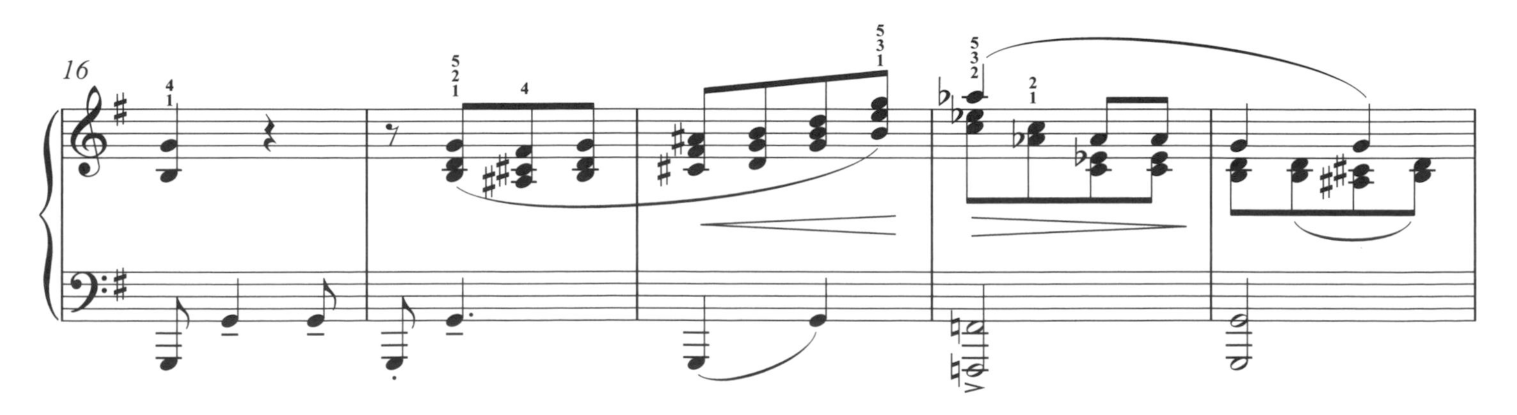

cresc.


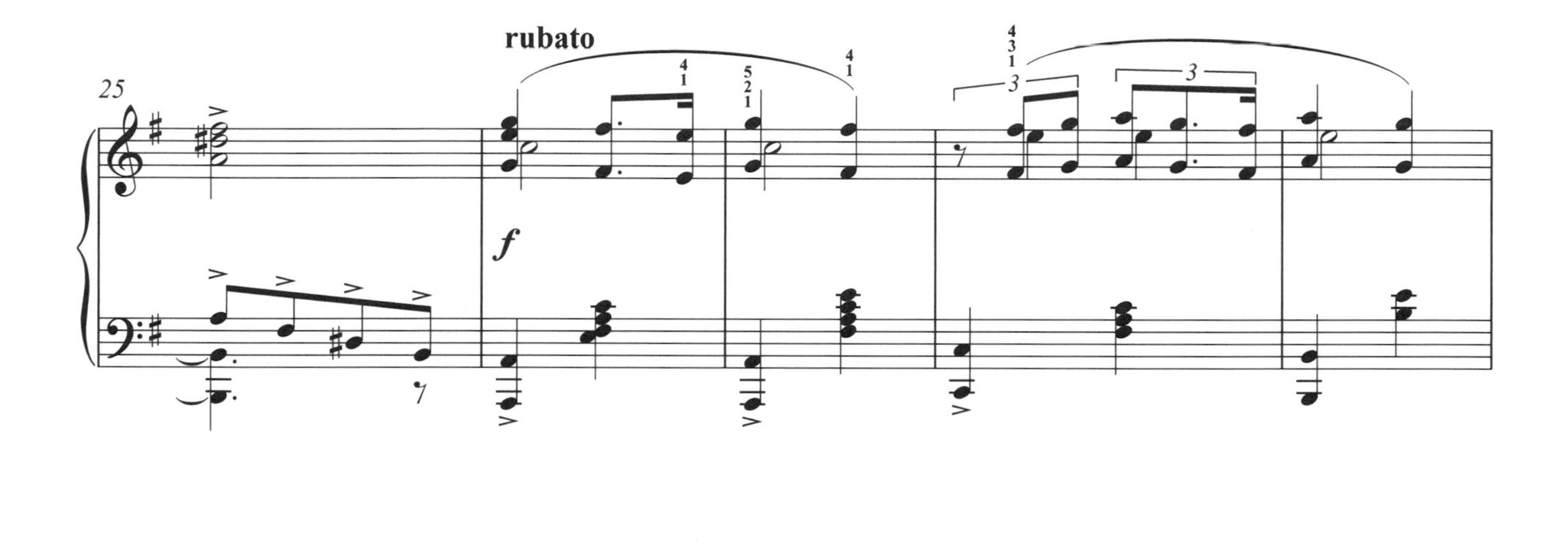

rubato
f


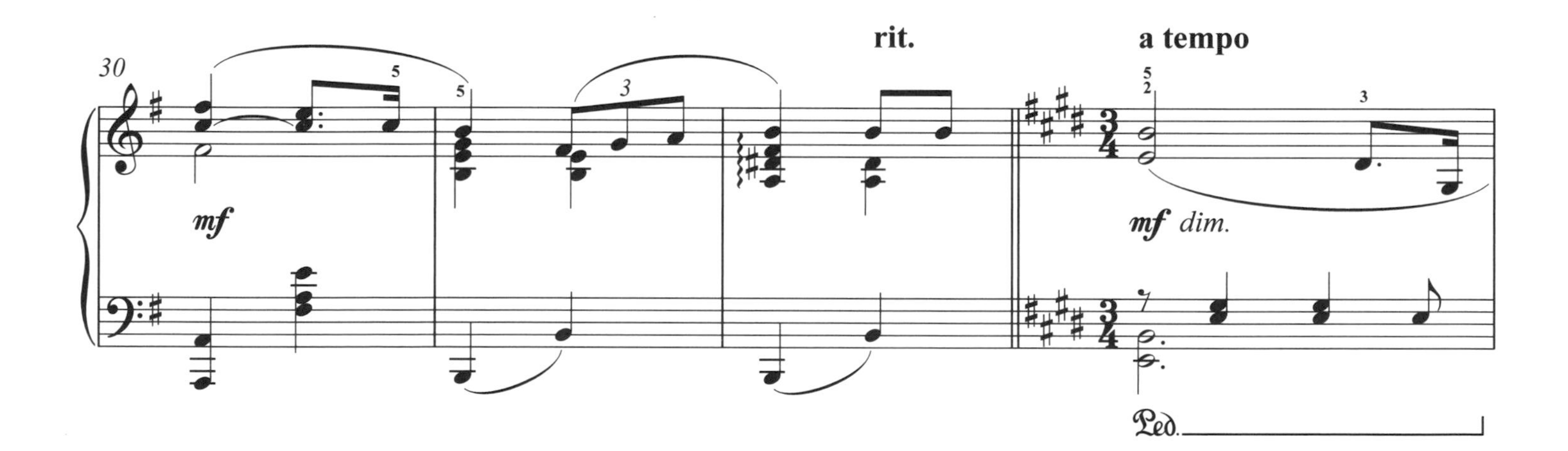

rit.
a tempo
mf
mf dim.
Ped.

p
pp
8vb

# VOI CHE SAPETE
## (FROM 'THE MARRIAGE OF FIGARO')

Composed by Wolfgang Amadeus Mozart
Arranged by Jack Long

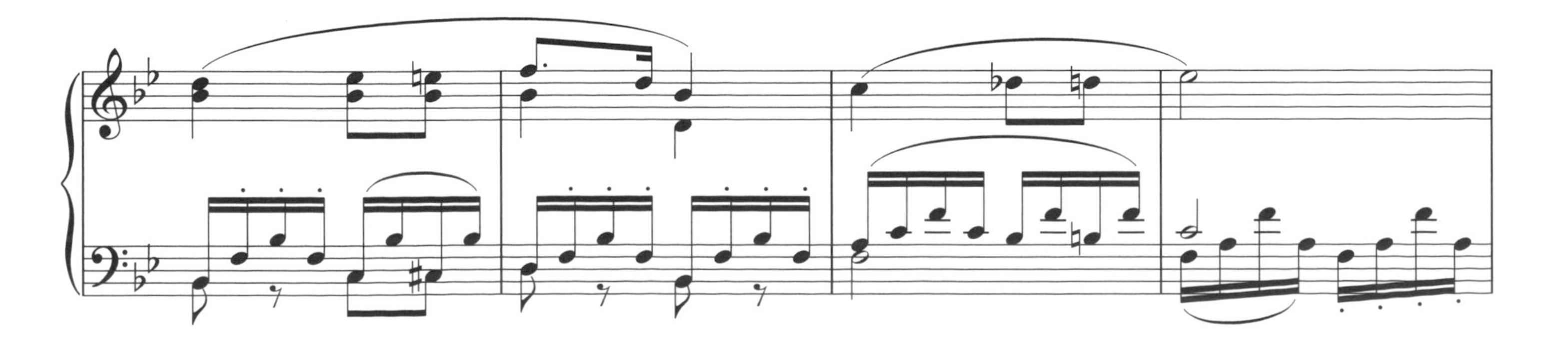

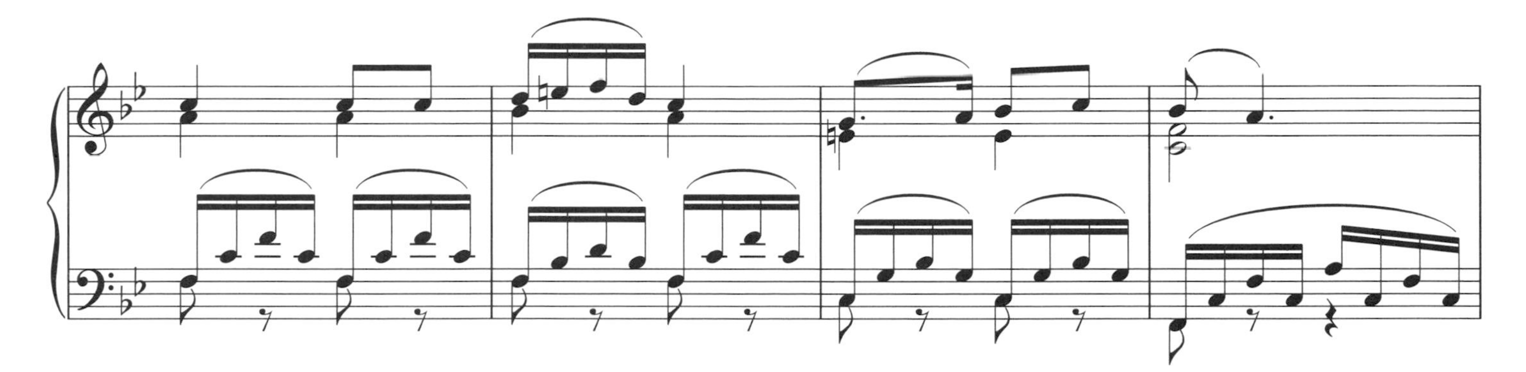

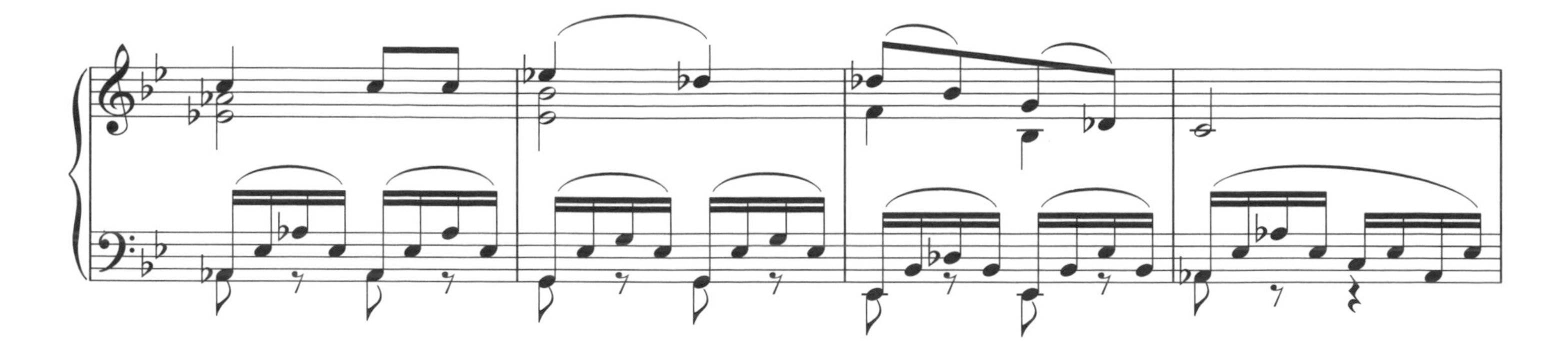

poco cresc.

(poco cresc.)
mp

poco rit.
a tempo
p

rit.
tr
tr

# WILLIAM TELL
## (OVERTURE: FINALE)

Composed by Gioachino Rossini

Arranged by Jeremy Birchall



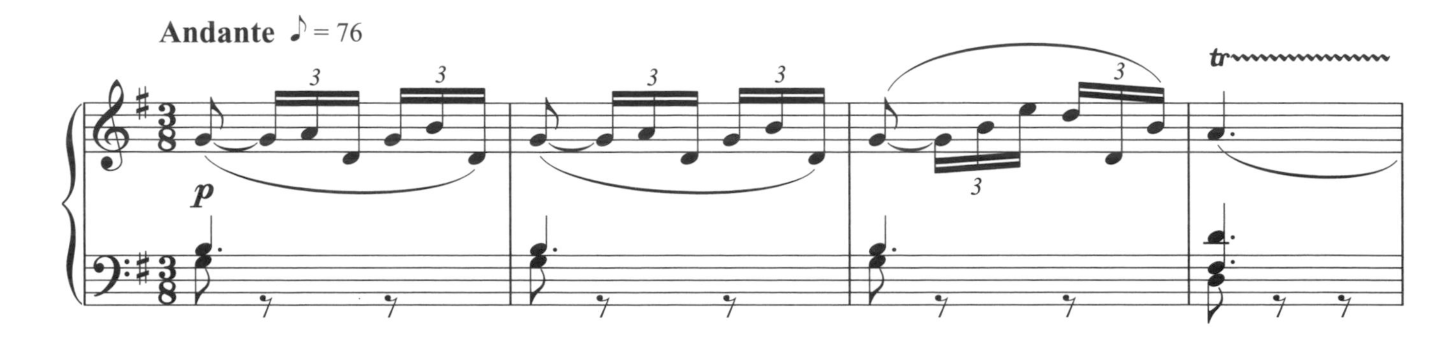


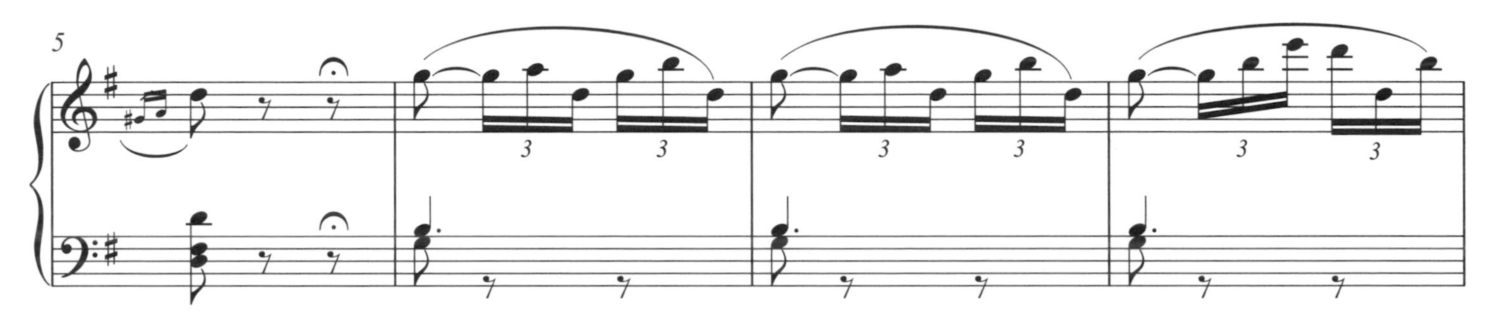


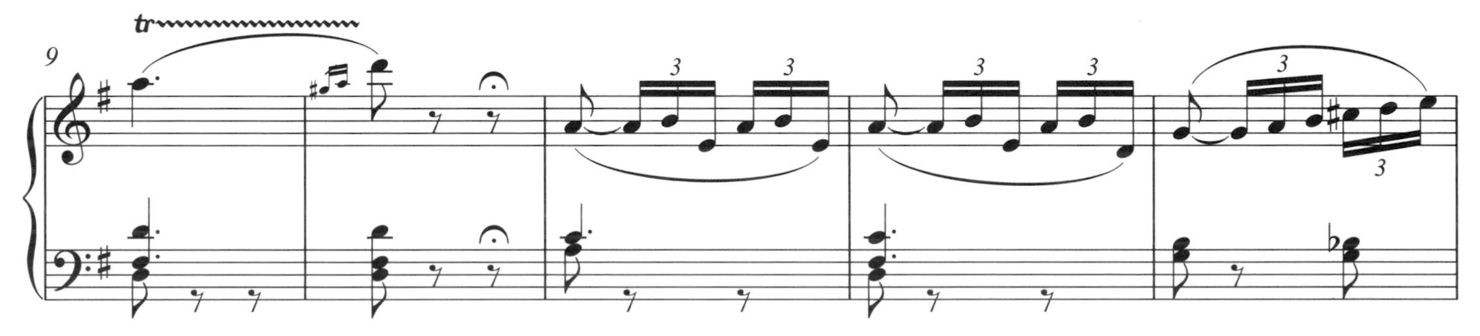


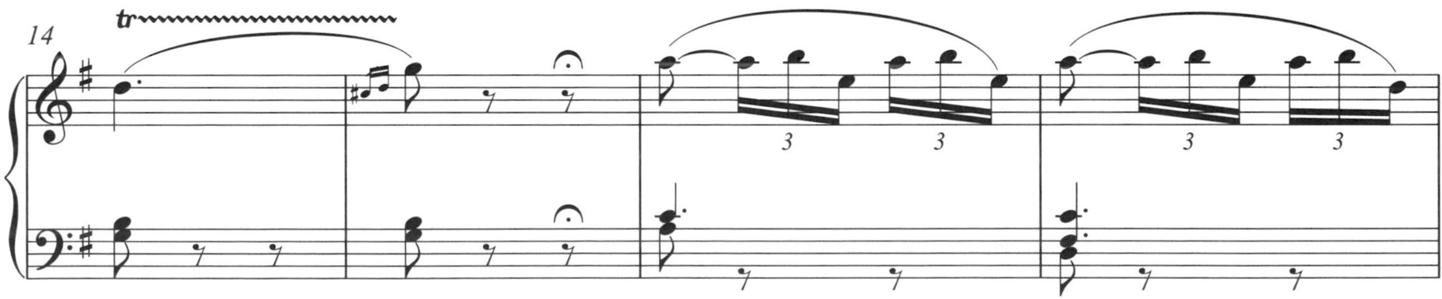

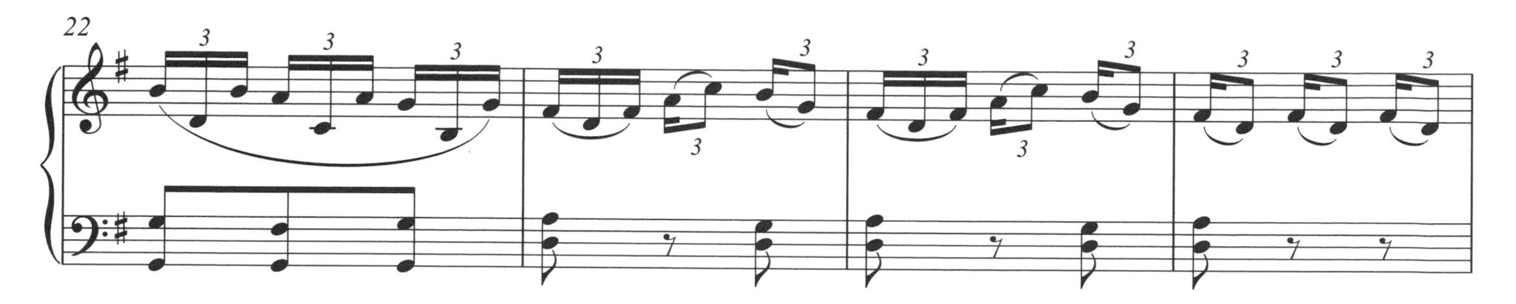
22
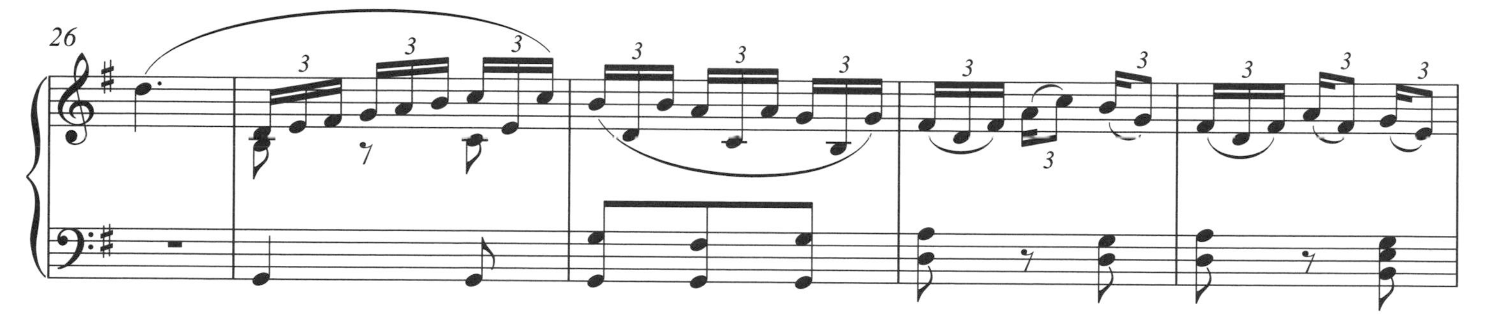
26
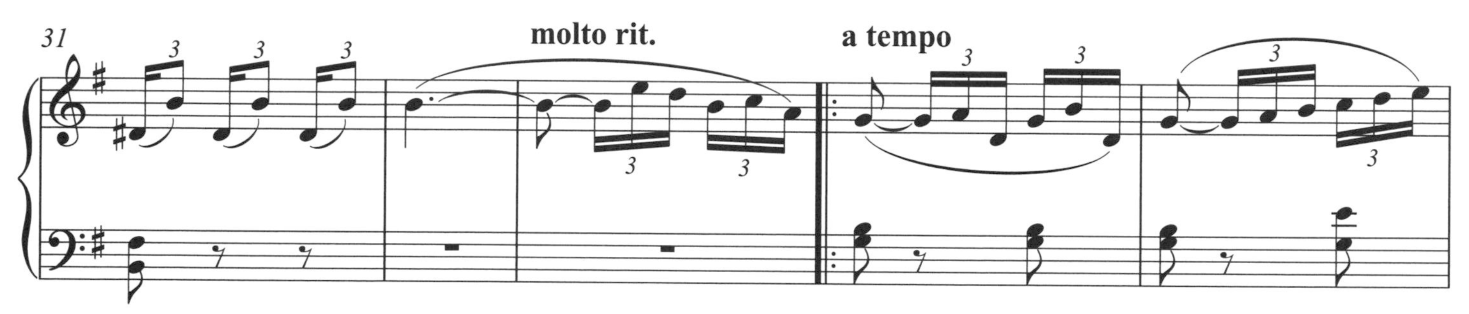
31
molto rit.
a tempo

36

41

46
Allegro Vivace ♩ = 152

51
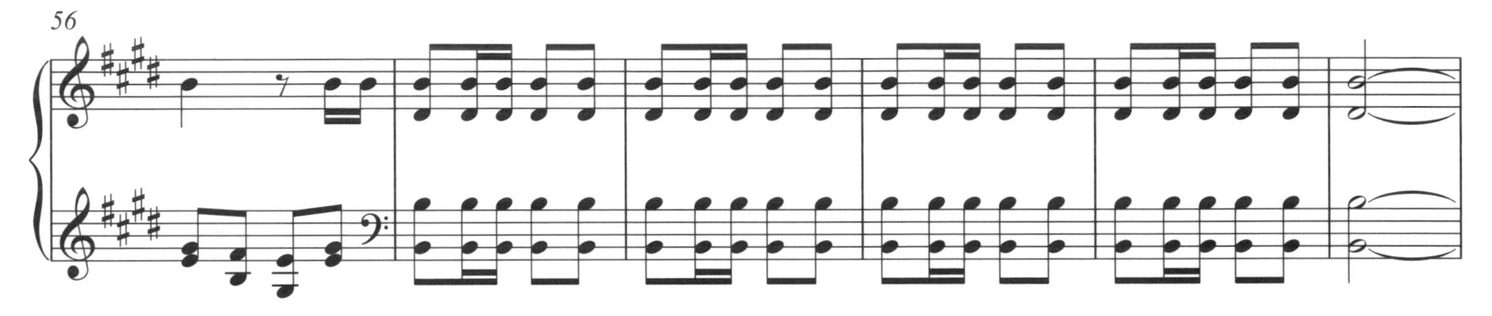
56
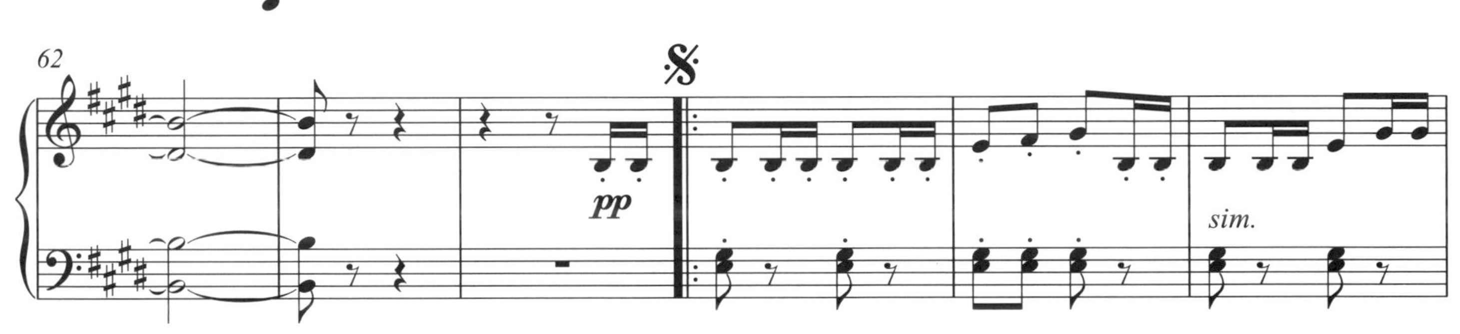
62
pp
sim.

To Coda
68
1.
2.
ff

74
f

80
1.
2.

86
D.S. al Coda
Coda

92
sim.
ff

98

103

108

114

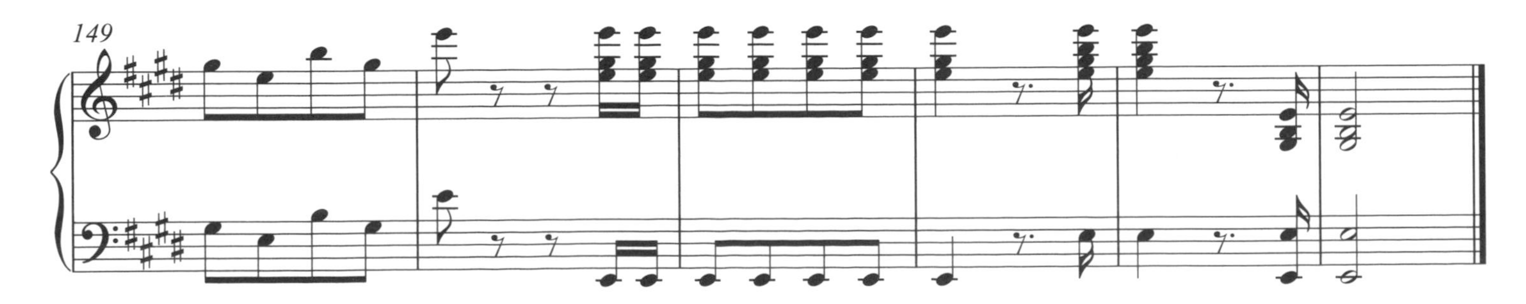


1 2 3 4 5 6 7 8 9